KNITTING
FOR BABIES

KNITTING FOR BABIES

From the Archives of the Lindberg Press

Complete Instructions for 36 Sweaters, Dresses,
Rompers and Other Projects

Edited by
Sondra R. Albert

DOVER PUBLICATIONS, INC.
NEW YORK

Published in Canada by General Publishing Company, Ltd., 30 Lesmill Road, Don Mills, Toronto, Ontario.

Knitting for Babies. Complete Instructions for 36 Sweaters, Dresses, Rompers and Other Projects, first published in 1981, is a collection of patterns from the archives of the Lindberg Press, Copenhagen, Denmark. The instructions have been prepared especially for this edition.

International Standard Book Number: 0-486-23953-5
Library of Congress Catalog Card Number: 80-68657

Manufactured in the United States of America
Dover Publications, Inc.
180 Varick Street
New York, N.Y. 10014

How to Follow the Pattern Directions

ASTERISK(*): When an * appears, complete the directions immediately following it, and then repeat those directions across the entire row or as many times as specified.

BRACKETS[ ]: When a series of directions is enclosed in brackets, work these directions the number of times specified, and then continue to work the rest of the row.

GAUGE: This is the number of stitches and/or rows per inch that must be worked to achieve the finished measurements specified in the instructions. Always test your own gauge before beginning a project. To do this, cast on approximately 20 stitches, using the yarn and needle size specified, and work in the pattern stitch specified for about 3 inches. Then measure how many stitches and rows you made per inch. If your swatch has more stitches and rows per inch than the gauge called for in the project instructions, your work is too tight and you

should use larger knitting needles; if you have fewer stitches and rows per inch than the project gauge, your work is too loose and you should change to smaller knitting needles.

ITALICS: Useful hints and additional information—for example, the total number of stitches to be worked across a given row—are noted in italics.

PARENTHESES ( ): Changes required for additional sizes are enclosed in parentheses. When no change is required to adapt the pattern to the additional sizes included, a single instruction is given that applies to all sizes.

WORK EVEN: When this phrase is used, it means you must continue to work on the same number of stitches without either increasing or decreasing.

Metric Conversion Chart

CONVERTING INCHES INTO MILLIMETERS AND CENTIMETERS

(Slightly rounded off for convenience)

inches	mm		cm	inches	cm	inches	cm	inches	cm
⅛	3mm			5	12.5	21	53.5	38	96.5
¼	6mm			5½	14	22	56	39	99
⅜	10mm	or	1cm	6	15	23	58.5	40	101.5
½	13mm	or	1.3cm	7	18	24	61	41	104
⅝	15mm	or	1.5cm	8	20.5	25	63.5	42	106.5
¾	20mm	or	2cm	9	23	26	66	43	109
⅞	22mm	or	2.2cm	10	25.5	27	68.5	44	112
1	25mm	or	2.5cm	11	28	28	71	45	114.5
1¼	32mm	or	3.2cm	12	30.5	29	73.5	46	117
1½	38mm	or	3.8cm	13	33	30	76	47	119.5
1¾	45mm	or	4.5cm	14	35.5	31	79	48	122
2	50mm	or	5cm	15	38	32	81.5	49	124.5
2½	65mm	or	6.5cm	16	40.5	33	84	50	127
3	75mm	or	7.5cm	17	43	34	86.5		
3½	90mm	or	9cm	18	46	35	89		
4	100mm	or	10cm	19	48.5	36	91.5		
4½	115mm	or	11.5cm	20	51	37	94		

mm—millimeters   cm—centimeters   m—meters

Knitting Needle Conversion Chart

BRITISH

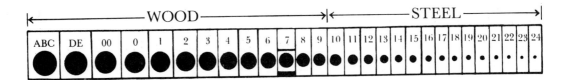

CONTINENTAL

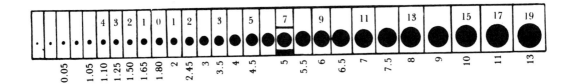

AMERICAN

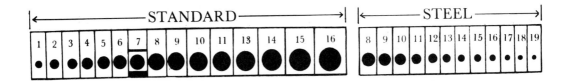

PUBLISHER'S NOTE

All needle sizes specified throughout this book are American
Standard sizes. Refer to the chart above to make any necessary
conversions.

Contents

KNITTING
FOR BABIES

Striped Ribbed Pullover, Pants, and Cap

SIZES: Directions are for size 6 months. Changes for sizes 12 and 18 months are given in parentheses. Pullover measures approximately 19 (20¼, 21) inches around chest. Cap measures approximately 16¼ (17¼, 18¼) inches around lower edge.

MATERIALS: Baby or fingering yarn, 6 (7, 7) ounces medium green, 2 (4, 4) ounces turquoise, 2 ounces dark brown. Knitting needles Nos. 2 and 3 (or size needed to obtain gauge). Three stitch holders. Large-eyed tapestry needle. Three small buttons. One-half yard ½-inch-wide elastic.

GAUGE: 8 stitches = 1 inch; 21 rows = 2 inches (ribbing, slightly stretched; No. 3 needles).

STRIPE PATTERN: Working in knit 2, purl 2 ribbing, work 4 rows turquoise, 4 rows green and 2 rows brown. Repeat these 10 rows for stripe pattern, cutting and joining colors as needed.

PULLOVER

BACK: Beginning at lower edge, with green and No. 2 needles, cast on 78 (82, 86) stitches. Work even in knit 2, purl 2 ribbing for 12 rows. Now change to No. 3 needles and work ribbing in stripe pattern until piece measures 6 (7, 8) inches or desired length to underarm, working last row on wrong side and finishing with a brown stripe if possible. Then cut brown, or color in use, attach green for remainder of piece and work as follows:
Shape Armholes: Continuing in ribbing with green, bind off 4 stitches at beginning of next 2 rows, 3 stitches at beginning of next 2 rows, 2 stitches at beginning of next 2 rows and 1 stitch at beginning of next 8 rows—*52 (56, 60) stitches.*
Divide for Center Back Opening: Next Row: Work first 26 (28, 30) stitches in ribbing; drop yarn without cutting it and attach another strand of green; with new strand, work in ribbing to end of row—*26 (28, 30) stitches each side.* Working both sides at same time with separate strands of green, work even in ribbing until armholes measure 3¼ (3¾, 4) inches.
Shape Shoulders: Continuing in ribbing and working both sides at same time with separate strands of green, at each armhole edge bind off 6 stitches once, 5 (6, 6) stitches once and 5 (5, 6) stitches once—*10 (11, 12) stitches each side.* Slip stitches remaining on each side onto stitch holders.

FRONT: Work as for back to underarm.
Shape Armholes: Continuing in ribbing with green,

bind off 4 stitches at beginning of next 2 rows, 3 stitches at beginning of next 2 rows, 2 stitches at beginning of next 2 rows and 1 stitch at beginning of next 8 rows—*52 (56, 60) stitches.* Then work even in ribbing until armholes measure 2 (2, 2¼) inches.
Shape Neck: Next Row: Work first 22 (24, 26) stitches in ribbing and then drop yarn without cutting it; slip next 8 stitches onto a stitch holder; attach another strand of green; with new strand, work remaining 22 (24, 26) stitches in ribbing. Working both sides at same time with separate strands of green, at each neck edge bind off 3 stitches once, 2 stitches once and 1 stitch 1 (2, 3) times—*16 (17, 18) stitches each side.* Then work both sides even in ribbing until armholes measure 3¼ (3¾, 4) inches.
Shape Shoulders: Continuing in ribbing and working both sides at same time with separate strands of green, at each armhole edge bind off 6 stitches once, 5 (6, 6) stitches once and 5 (5, 6) stitches once.

RIGHT SLEEVE: Beginning at lower edge, with green and No. 2 needles, cast on 42 (44, 46) stitches. Work even in knit 2, purl 2 ribbing for 12 rows. Now change to No. 3 needles and work ribbing in stripe pattern, increasing 1 stitch at each side every 6 rows 8 times—*58 (60, 62) stitches.* Then work even in ribbing and stripe pattern until piece measures 5¾ (7, 7¾) inches or desired length to underarm, working last row on wrong side.
Shape Cap: Continuing in ribbing and stripe pattern, bind off 3 stitches at beginning of next 2 rows—*52 (54, 56) stitches.* Then decrease 1 stitch at each side every other row 17 times, working the decreases on the right side of the piece—*18 (20, 22) stitches.* Now bind off 2 stitches at beginning of next 2 rows and 3 stitches at beginning of next 2 rows—*8 (10, 12) stitches.* Bind off remaining stitches.

LEFT SLEEVE: Work as for right sleeve.

FINISHING: Weave all remaining yarn ends into back of work. Block pieces lightly if necessary. Working from wrong side, seam front and back sections together at shoulders, sew sleeves to body, and then sew side and sleeve underarm seams.

NECKBAND: Working from right side of garment, with green and No. 2 needles, knit the 10 (11, 12) stitches from left back stitch holder, pick up 16 (18, 20) stitches along left front neck edge, knit the 8 stitches from front neck stitch holder, pick up 16 (18, 20) stitches along right front neck edge, and then knit the 10 (11, 12) stitches from right back stitch holder—*60 (66, 72) stitches.* Then work even in knit 2, purl 2 ribbing for 8 rows.

3

Bind off loosely in ribbing from wrong side of work.

Sew three yarn loops evenly spaced along one edge of center back opening. Sew buttons in position along opposite edge of opening.

PANTS

LEFT LEG: Beginning at lower edge, with green and No. 2 needles, cast on 78 (82, 86) stitches. Work even in knit 2, purl 2 ribbing for 4 rows. Then change to No. 3 needles and continue in ribbing pattern as established, increasing 1 stitch at each side every 4 rows 4 times—*86 (90, 94) stitches.*

Shape Crotch: Next Row (right side): Bind off first 5 stitches (*center back edge*), work remaining stitches in ribbing pattern as established—*81 (85, 89) stitches.* Mark center back edge by inserting a safety pin in first bound-off stitch.

Next Row (wrong side): Bind off first 3 stitches (*center front edge*), work in ribbing pattern across row—*78 (82, 86) stitches.*

Next Row: Bind off first 4 stitches (*center back edge*), work in ribbing pattern across row—*74 (78, 82) stitches.*

Next Row: Bind off first 2 stitches (*center front edge*), work in ribbing pattern across row—*72 (76, 80) stitches.*

Next Row: Bind off first 3 stitches (*center back edge*), work in ribbing pattern across row—*69 (73, 77) stitches.*

Next Row: Bind off first stitch (*center front edge*), work in ribbing pattern across row—*68 (72, 76) stitches.*

Next Row: Bind off first 2 stitches (*center back edge*), work in ribbing pattern across row—*66 (70, 74) stitches.*

Next Row: Bind off first stitch (*center front edge*), work in ribbing pattern across row—*65 (69, 73) stitches.*

Next Row: Work first 2 stitches together (*center back edge*), work in ribbing pattern across row. Work next 3 rows even in ribbing pattern. Repeat these 4 rows 3 times—*61 (65, 69) stitches.* Then work even in ribbing pattern until piece measures 4¾ (5, 5½) inches from first bound-off row of crotch, working last row on wrong side (*finish at center back edge*).

Shape Back (Short Rows): Row 1: Starting at center back edge, work first 28 (32, 36) stitches in ribbing pattern, turn (*do not work remaining stitches of row*).

Row 2: Slip first stitch, work remaining 27 (31, 35) stitches in ribbing pattern.

Row 3: Work first 21 (24, 27) stitches in ribbing pattern, turn (*do not work remaining stitches of row*).

Row 4: Slip first stitch, work remaining 20 (23, 26) stitches in ribbing pattern.

Row 5: Work first 14 (16, 18) stitches in ribbing pattern, turn (*do not work remaining stitches of row*).

Row 6: Slip first stitch, work remaining 13 (15, 17) stitches in ribbing pattern.

Row 7: Work first 7 (8, 9) stitches in ribbing pattern, turn (*do not work remaining stitches of row*).

Row 8: Slip first stitch, work remaining 6 (7, 8) stitches in ribbing pattern.

Waistband: Next Row: Change to No. 2 needles and work in ribbing pattern across entire row, working each slipped stitch together with stitch directly below it—*61 (65, 69) stitches.* Then work even in ribbing for 1 inch. Bind off loosely in ribbing.

RIGHT LEG: Beginning at lower edge, with green and No. 2 needles, cast on 78 (82, 86) stitches. Work even in knit 2, purl 2 ribbing for 4 rows. Then change to No. 3 needles and continue in ribbing pattern as established, increasing 1 stitch at each side every 4 rows 4 times—*86 (90, 94) stitches*

Shape Crotch: Next Row (right side): Bind off first 3 stitches (*center front edge*), work remaining stitches in ribbing pattern as established—*83 (87, 91) stitches.*

Next Row (wrong side): Bind off first 5 stitches (*center back edge*), mark center back edge by inserting a safety pin in first bound-off stitch of row, then work in ribbing across row—*78 (82, 86) stitches.*

Next Row: Bind off first 2 stitches (*center front edge*), work in ribbing pattern across row—*76 (80, 84) stitches.*

Next Row: Bind off first 4 stitches (*center back edge*), work in ribbing pattern across row—*72 (76, 80) stitches.*

Next Row: Bind off first stitch (*center front edge*), work in ribbing pattern across row—*71 (75, 79) stitches.*

Next Row: Bind off first 3 stitches (*center back edge*), work in ribbing pattern across row—*68 (72, 76) stitches.*

Next Row: Bind off first stitch (*center front edge*), work in ribbing pattern across row—*67 (71, 75) stitches.*

Next Row: Bind off first 2 stitches (*center back edge*), work in ribbing pattern across row—*65 (69, 73) stitches.*

Next Row: Work in ribbing pattern to last 2 stitches, work last 2 stitches together (*center back edge*). Work next 3 rows even in ribbing pattern. Repeat these 4 rows 3 times—*61 (65, 69) stitches.* Then work even in ribbing pattern until piece measures 4¾ (5, 5½) inches from first bound-off row of crotch, working last row on the right side of the piece (*finish at center back edge*).

Shape Back (Short Rows): Row 1: Starting at center back edge, work first 28 (32, 36) stitches in ribbing pattern, turn (*do not work remaining stitches of row*).

Row 2: Slip first stitch, work remaining 27 (31, 35) stitches in ribbing pattern.

Row 3: Work first 21 (24, 27) stitches in ribbing pattern, turn (*do not work remaining stitches of row*).

Row 4: Slip first stitch, work remaining 20 (23, 26) stitches in ribbing pattern.

Row 5: Work first 14 (16, 18) stitches in ribbing pattern, turn (*do not work remaining stitches of row*).

Row 6: Slip first stitch, work remaining 13 (15, 17) stitches in ribbing pattern.

Row 7: Work first 7 (8, 9) stitches in ribbing pattern, turn (*do not work remaining stitches of row*).

Row 8: Slip first stitch, work remaining 6 (7, 8) stitches in ribbing pattern.

Waistband: Next Row: Change to No. 2 needles and work in ribbing pattern across entire row, working each slipped stitch together with stitch directly below it—*61 (65, 69) stitches.* Then work even in ribbing for 1 inch. Bind off loosely in ribbing.

FINISHING: Weave all remaining yarn ends into back of work. Block pieces lightly if necessary. Working from wrong side, sew short inseam of each leg, and then sew legs together. Cut elastic to fit, stitch the ends together, and sew to inside of waistband.

CAP

Beginning at lower edge, with green and No. 2 needles, cast on 134 (142, 150) stitches. Work even in knit 2, purl 2 ribbing for 3½ inches. Then change to No. 3 needles and work ribbing in stripe pattern until piece measures 7 (7½, 8) inches, working last row on wrong side.

Next Row (right side): Knit 2 together; * purl 2, knit 2 together; repeat from * across row—*100 (106, 112) stitches.*

Next Row (wrong side): Purl 1; * knit 2 together, purl 1; repeat from * across row—*67 (71, 75) stitches.*

Next Row: Knit 3 together; * purl 1, knit 3 together; repeat from * across row—*33 (35, 37) stitches.* Cut yarn, leaving a 12-inch end.

Thread yarn end onto a blunt-tipped tapestry needle and draw through all stitches on knitting needle. Pull tight and fasten securely on wrong side of work.

FINISHING: Weave all remaining yarn ends into back of work. Sew side edges together for center back seam; start at lower edge and sew first 2 inches from right side, then complete seam from wrong side. Turn up lower edge 2 inches to form a cuff. Make a pompon with green yarn and sew to top of cap.

6 *Raglan Cardigan and Peaked Cap*

Raglan Cardigan and Peaked Cap

SIZES: Directions are for size 3 months. Changes for sizes 6, 9, 12 and 15 months are given in parentheses. Cardigan measures approximately 18¾ (19½, 20¼, 21, 22) inches around chest.

MATERIALS: Baby or fingering yarn, 6 (6, 7, 7, 7) ounces coral. Knitting needles Nos. 2 and 3 (or size needed to obtain gauge). Crochet hook size B. Large-eyed tapestry needle. Six buttons.

GAUGE: 15 stitches = 2 inches; 10 rows = 1 inch (stockinette stitch, No. 3 needles).

CARDIGAN

BACK: Beginning at lower edge, with No. 2 needles, cast on 74 (78, 82, 84, 86) stitches. Work even in knit 1, purl 1 ribbing for 1 inch. Change to No. 3 needles and work in stockinette stitch (*knit 1 row, purl 1 row*) until piece measures 4¾ (5½, 6¼, 7, 7¾) inches or desired length to underarm, finishing with a purl row.
Shape Raglan Armholes: Bind off 3 stitches at beginning of next 2 rows—*68 (72, 76, 78, 80) stitches.* Then decrease 1 stitch at each side every other row 20 (21, 22, 23, 24) times, working the decreases on the knit rows—*28 (30, 32, 32, 32) stitches.* Bind off.

RIGHT FRONT: Beginning at lower edge, with No 2 needles, cast on 35 (37, 39, 40, 41) stitches. Work even in knit 1, purl 1 ribbing for 1 inch. Then change to No. 3 needles and work as follows:

PATTERN: Row 1 (right side): Knit 3, place a marker on needle, [purl 2, knit 5] 2 times, purl 2, place a marker on needle, knit remaining 16 (18, 20, 21, 22) stitches.
Row 2: Purl to first marker, slip marker, [knit 2, purl 5] 2 times, knit 2, slip marker, purl remaining 3 stitches.
Row 3: Knit 3, slip marker, [purl 2, yarn over, knit 1, knit 3 together, knit 1, yarn over] 2 times, purl 2, slip marker, knit remaining 16 (18, 20, 21, 22) stitches.
Row 4: Purl to first marker, slip marker, [knit 2, purl 5] 2 times, knit 2, slip marker, purl remaining 3 stitches.
Row 5: Knit 3, slip marker, [purl 2, knit 1, yarn over, knit 3 together, yarn over, knit 1] 2 times, purl 2, slip marker, knit remaining 16 (18, 20, 21, 22) stitches.
Row 6: Purl to first marker, slip marker, [knit 2, purl 5] 2 times, knit 2, slip marker, purl remaining 3 stitches.
Row 7: Knit 3, slip marker, [purl 2, knit 2, yarn over, knit 2 together, knit 1] 2 times, purl 2, slip marker, knit remaining 16 (18, 20, 21, 22) stitches.
Row 8: Purl to first marker, slip marker, [knit 2, purl 5] 2 times, knit 2, slip marker, purl remaining 3 stitches.
Repeat Rows 1–8 for pattern until piece measures same as back to underarm, working last row on right side.
Shape Raglan Armhole: Continuing in pattern as established, bind off 3 stitches at beginning of next row (*armhole edge*)—*32 (34, 36, 37, 38) stitches.* Then decrease 1 stitch at armhole edge every other row 11 (12, 13, 13, 14) times, working the decreases on the right side of the piece—*21 (22, 23, 24, 24) stitches.* Work next row even on wrong side.
Shape Neck: Continuing in pattern as established, at neck edge bind off 7 (8, 9, 9, 9) stitches once, 2 stitches once and 1 stitch 3 times; at same time, continue to decrease 1 stitch at armhole edge every other row as before until only 2 stitches remain. Bind off.

LEFT FRONT: Beginning at lower edge, with No. 2 needles, cast on 35 (37, 39, 40, 41) stitches. Work even in knit 1, purl 1 ribbing for 1 inch. Then change to No. 3 needles and work as follows:

PATTERN: Row 1 (right side): Knit first 16 (18, 20, 21, 22) stitches, place a marker on needle, [purl 2, knit 5] 2 times, purl 2, place a marker on needle, knit remaining 3 stitches.
Row 2: Purl 3, slip marker, [knit 2, purl 5] 2 times, knit 2, slip marker, purl remaining 16 (18, 20, 21, 22) stitches.
Row 3: Knit to first marker, slip marker, [purl 2, yarn over, knit 1, knit 3 together, knit 1, yarn over] 2 times, purl 2, slip marker, knit remaining 3 stitches.
Row 4: Purl 3, slip marker, [knit 2, purl 5] 2 times, knit 2, slip marker, purl remaining 16 (18, 20, 21, 22) stitches.
Row 5: Knit to first marker, slip marker, [purl 2, knit 1, yarn over, knit 3 together, yarn over, knit 1] 2 times, purl 2, slip marker, knit remaining 3 stitches.
Row 6: Purl 3, slip marker, [knit 2, purl 5] 2 times, knit 2, slip marker, purl remaining 16 (18, 20, 21, 22) stitches.
Row 7: Knit to first marker, slip marker, [purl 2, knit 2, yarn over, knit 2 together, knit 1] 2 times, purl 2, slip marker, knit remaining 3 stitches.
Row 8: Purl 3, slip marker, [knit 2, purl 5] 2 times, knit 2, slip marker, purl remaining 16 (18, 20, 21, 22) stitches. Repeat Rows 1–8 for pattern until piece measures same as back to underarm, working last row on wrong side.
Shape Raglan Armhole: Continuing in pattern as established, bind off 3 stitches at beginning of next row (*armhole edge*)—*32 (34, 36, 37, 38) stitches.* Then decrease 1 stitch at armhole edge every other row 11 (12, 13, 13, 14) times, working the decreases on the right side of the piece—*21 (22, 23, 24, 24) stitches.*
Shape Neck: Continuing in pattern as established, at

neck edge bind off 7 (8, 9, 9, 9) stitches once, 2 stitches once and 1 stitch 3 times; at same time, continue to decrease 1 stitch at armhole edge every other row as before until only 2 stitches remain. Bind off.

RIGHT SLEEVE: Beginning at lower edge, with No. 2 needles, cast on 39 (41, 41, 43, 43) stitches. Work in knit 1, purl 1 ribbing for 2 inches, increasing 4 stitches evenly spaced across last row—*43 (45, 45, 47, 47) stitches.* Then change to No. 3 needles and work as follows:

PATTERN: Row 1 (right side): Knit first 17 (18, 18, 19, 19) stitches, place a marker on needle, purl 2, knit 5, purl 2, place a marker on needle, knit to end of row.
Row 2: Purl to first marker, slip marker, knit 2, purl 5, knit 2, slip marker, purl to end of row.
Row 3: Knit to first marker, slip marker, purl 2, yarn over, knit 1, knit 3 together, knit 1, yarn over, purl 2, slip marker, knit to end of row.
Row 4: Purl to first marker, slip marker, knit 2, purl 5, knit 2, slip marker, purl to end of row.
Row 5: Knit to first marker, purl 2, knit 1, yarn over, knit 3 together, yarn over, knit 1, purl 2, slip marker, knit to end of row.
Row 6: Purl to first marker, slip marker, knit 2, purl 5, knit 2, slip marker, purl to end of row.
Row 7: Knit to first marker, slip marker, purl 2, knit 2, yarn over, knit 2 together, knit 1, purl 2, slip marker, knit to end of row.
Row 8: Purl to first marker, slip marker, knit 2, purl 5, knit 2, slip marker, purl to end of row. Repeat Rows 1–8 for pattern, increasing 1 stitch at each side every 6 rows 7 (7, 8, 8, 9) times—*57 (59, 61, 63, 65) stitches.* Continuing in pattern as established, work even until piece measures 6¼ (7, 7¾, 8½, 9¼) inches or desired length to underarm, working last row on wrong side.
Shape Raglan Cap: Continuing in pattern as established, bind off 3 stitches at beginning of next 2 rows—*51 (53, 55, 57, 59) stitches.* Then decrease 1 stitch at each side every other row 18 (19, 20, 21, 22) times, working the decreases on the right side of the piece—*15 stitches.*
Next Row (wrong side): Work even in pattern across row.
Next Row (right side): Bind off first 4 stitches (*front edge*), work in pattern to last 2 stitches, knit last 2 stitches together—*10 stitches.*
Next Row: Work even in pattern across row.
Next Row: Bind off first 4 stitches (*front edge*), work in pattern to last 2 stitches, knit last 2 stitches together—*5 stitches.*
Next Row: Work even in pattern across row. Bind off remaining 5 stitches.

LEFT SLEEVE: Work as for right sleeve to underarm.
Shape Raglan Cap: Continuing in pattern as established, bind off 3 stitches at beginning of next 2 rows—*51 (53, 55, 57, 59) stitches.* Then decrease 1 stitch at each side every other row 18 (19, 20, 21, 22) times, working the decreases on the right side of the piece—*15 stitches.*
Next Row (wrong side): Bind off first 4 stitches (*front edge*), work remaining 10 stitches in pattern—*11 stitches.*
Next Row (right side): Knit first 2 stitches together, work remaining 9 stitches in pattern—*10 stitches.*
Next Row: Bind off first 4 stitches (*front edge*), work remaining 5 stitches in pattern—*6 stitches.*
Next Row: Knit first 2 stitches together, work remaining 4 stitches in pattern—*5 stitches.* Bind off.

FINISHING: Weave all remaining yarn ends into back of work. Block pieces lightly if necessary. Working from wrong side, sew sleeves to front and back sections. Then sew side and sleeve underarm seams.

NECKBAND: Working from right side of garment, with No. 2 needles, pick up 75 (77, 81, 83, 85) stitches around neck edge. Work even in knit 1, purl 1 ribbing for 6 rows. Bind off in ribbing from wrong side of work.

LEFT FRONT BAND: Working from right side of garment, with No. 2 needles, pick up stitches evenly along left front edge. Work even in knit 1, purl 1 ribbing for 1 inch. Bind off in ribbing from wrong side of work.

RIGHT FRONT BAND: Work as for left front band until ribbing measures ½ inch. With pins, mark position of six buttonholes evenly spaced along front edge, inserting top pin ¾ inch from neck edge and bottom pin ¾ inch from lower edge.
Next Row (Buttonhole Row): * Work in ribbing pattern as established to 1 stitch before pin marker, bind off next 2 stitches; repeat from * 5 times; work in ribbing to end of row.
Next Row: * Work in ribbing pattern as established to bound-off stitches, cast on 2 stitches directly over bound-off stitches; repeat from * 5 times; work in ribbing to end of row. Then work even in ribbing until band measures 1 inch. Bind off in ribbing from wrong side of work.
Sew buttons in position on left front band.
(NOTE: For a boy's sweater, make buttonholes on left front band instead of on right front band.)

PEAKED CAP

With No. 3 needles, cast on 36 (38, 39, 40, 41) stitches. Work in garter stitch (*knit each row*) as follows:
Row 1: Knit even across row.
Next Row: Knit 2, knit 2 together (*1 decrease made*), knit to last 3 stitches, knit in front and in back of next stitch (*1 increase made*), knit 2. Knit even across next row. Repeat these 2 rows 17 (18, 19, 20, 21) times.
Next Row: Knit 2, knit in front and in back of next stitch (*1 increase made*), knit to last 4 stitches, knit 2 together (*1 decrease made*), knit 2. Knit even across next row. Repeat these 2 rows 17 (18, 19, 20, 21) times.
Next Row: Knit 2, knit 2 together (*1 decrease made*), knit to last 3 stitches, knit in front and in back of next stitch

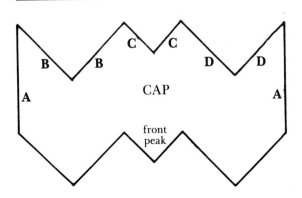

ASSEMBLING THE CAP. Sew together corresponding edges (indicated by the same letter).

(*1 increase made*), knit 2. Knit even across next row. Repeat these 2 rows 8 (10, 11, 12, 13) times.

Next Row: Knit 2, knit in front and in back of next stitch (*1 increase made*), knit to last 4 stitches, knit 2 together (*1 decrease made*), knit 2. Knit even across next row. Repeat these 2 rows 8 (10, 11, 12, 13) times.

Next Row: Knit 2, knit 2 together (*1 decrease made*), knit to last 3 stitches, knit in front and in back of next stitch (*1 increase made*), knit 2. Knit even across next row. Repeat these 2 rows 17 (18, 19, 20, 21) times.

Next Row: Knit 2, knit in front and in back of next stitch (*1 increase made*), knit to last 4 stitches, knit 2 together (*1 decrease made*), knit 2. Knit even across next row. Repeat these 2 rows 17 (18, 19, 20, 21) times. Bind off all stitches.

FINISHING: Weave all remaining yarn ends into back of work. Working from wrong side, seam back and side edges together (*see diagram*). Make ties for the cap by crocheting two 15-inch chains, using doubled strands of yarn. Sew ties to cap at sides. Make a small pompon and sew to top of cap.

Long-Sleeved Dress and Pants

SIZES: Directions are for size 3 months. Changes for sizes 6, 9, 12 and 15 months are given in parentheses. Dress measures approximately 18 (18¾, 19½, 20¼, 21½) inches around chest and 9¾ (10¾, 11¾, 12½, 14) inches from shoulder to bottom edge.

MATERIALS: Baby or fingering yarn, 6 ounces pink, 2 ounces blue. Knitting needles Nos. 3 and 4 (or size needed to obtain gauge). Crochet hook size B. Large-eyed tapestry needle. Three small buttons. Two-thirds yard ½-inch-wide elastic.

GAUGE: 7 stitches = 1 inch; 9 rows = 1 inch (stockinette stitch, No. 4 needles).

STRIPE PATTERN: Working in stockinette stitch (*knit 1 row, purl 1 row*), work 2 rows blue and 2 rows pink. Repeat these 4 rows for pattern, carrying color not in use at side of work.

DRESS

BACK: Beginning at lower edge, with pink and No. 3 needles, cast on 104 (108, 110, 118, 124) stitches. Work even in garter stitch (*knit each row*) for 7 rows. Change to No. 3 needles and work in stockinette stitch (*knit 1 row, purl 1 row*) until piece measures 5 (5¾, 6½, 7½, 8½) inches, finishing with a purl row.
Next Row (right side): Knit first 14 (14, 15, 15, 16) stitches; * knit 2, knit 2 together; repeat from * to last 14 (14, 15, 15, 16) stitches; knit remaining 14 (14, 15, 15, 16) stitches—*85 (88, 90, 96, 101) stitches.*
Next Row (wrong side): Purl first 14 (14, 15, 15, 16) stitches; * purl 1, purl 2 together; repeat from * to last 14 (14, 15, 15, 16) stitches; purl remaining 14 (14, 15, 15, 16) stitches—*66 (68, 70, 74, 78) stitches.* Then change to stripe pattern and work even until piece measures 5¾ (6½, 7½, 8¼, 9½) inches or desired length to underarm, finishing with a purl row.
Shape Raglan Armholes: Continuing in stripe pattern as established, bind off 3 stitches at beginning of next 2 rows—*60 (62, 64, 68, 72) stitches.* Then decrease 1 stitch at each side every other row 18 (19, 20, 21, 22) times, working the decreases on the knit rows—*24 (24, 24, 26, 28) stitches.* Bind off.

FRONT: Work as for back to underarm.
Shape Raglan Armholes: Continuing in stripe pattern as established, bind off 3 stitches at beginning of next 2 rows—*60 (62, 64, 68, 72) stitches.* Then decrease 1 stitch at each side every other row 10 (11, 12, 13, 13) times—*40 (40, 40, 42, 44) stitches.* Purl next row.

Shape Neck: Next Row (right side): Continuing in stripe pattern, knit 2 together, knit 11; drop yarn without cutting it and attach another strand of same color; with new strand, bind off next 14 (14, 14, 16, 18) stitches, knit to last 2 stitches, knit last 2 stitches together—*12 stitches each side.* Working both sides at same time with separate strands of yarn, at each neck edge bind off 2 stitches once and 1 stitch 3 times; at same time, continue to decrease 1 stitch at each armhole edge every other row as before until only 2 stitches remain on each side. Bind off.

RIGHT SLEEVE: Beginning at lower edge, with pink and No. 3 needles, cast on 40 (40, 42, 42, 44) stitches. Work even in garter stitch for 7 rows. Change to No. 4 needles and work stripe pattern in stockinette stitch, increasing 1 stitch at each side every 6 rows 6 (7, 7, 8, 8) times—*52 (54, 56, 58, 60) stitches.* Then work even in stripe pattern until piece measures 5½ (5¾, 6¼, 7, 7¾) inches or desired length to underarm, finishing with a purl row. (*NOTE: Be careful to match color of stripe on sleeve with color on front and back sections at underarm.*)
Shape Raglan Cap: Continuing in stripe pattern as established, bind off 3 stitches at beginning of next 2 rows—*46 (48, 50, 52, 54) stitches.* Then decrease 1 stitch at each side every other row 16 (17, 18, 19, 20) times, working the decreases on the knit rows—*14 stitches.* Purl next row.
Next Row (right side): Bind off first 4 stitches (*front edge*), knit 7, knit last 2 stitches together—*9 stitches.*
Next Row (wrong side): Purl even across row.
Next Row: Bind off first 4 stitches (*front edge*), knit 2, knit last 2 stitches together—*4 stitches.*
Next Row: Purl even across row. Bind off.

LEFT SLEEVE: Work as for right sleeve to underarm.
Shape Raglan Cap: Continuing in stripe pattern as established, bind off 3 stitches at beginning of next 2 rows—*46 (48, 50, 52, 54) stitches.* Then decrease 1 stitch at each side every other row 16 (17, 18, 19, 20) times, working the decreases on the knit rows—*14 stitches.*
Next Row (wrong side): Bind off first 4 stitches (*front edge*), purl remaining 9 stitches—*10 stitches.*
Next Row (right side): Knit first 2 stitches together, knit remaining 8 stitches—*9 stitches.*
Next Row: Bind off first 4 stitches (*front edge*), purl remaining 4 stitches—*5 stitches.*
Next Row: Knit first 2 stitches together, knit remaining 3 stitches—*4 stitches.* Bind off.

FINISHING: Weave all remaining yarn ends into back of work. Block pieces lightly if necessary. Working from wrong side, sew sleeves to front and back sections, leaving approximately 3 inches open at neck edge of left back raglan seam. Then sew side and sleeve underarm seams.

NECKBAND: Working from right side of garment, with pink and No. 3 needles, pick up 66 (68, 70, 74, 76) stitches around neck edge, starting and ending at open portion of left back raglan seam. Then work in garter stitch as follows:

Next Row (wrong side): Knit even across row.

Next Row (right side): Knit, decreasing 4 stitches evenly across row—*62 (64, 66, 70, 72) stitches.* Repeat these 2 rows 3 times—*50 (52, 54, 58, 60) stitches.* Bind off loosely.

With pink and size B crochet hook, work 1 row of single crochet stitches around edge of back opening, crocheting three chain-stitch loops evenly spaced along one side of opening. Sew buttons in position along opposite side of opening.

PANTS

FRONT: Beginning at lower edge of crotch, with pink and No. 4 needles, cast on 18 (18, 20, 20, 22) stitches. Work even in stockinette stitch (*knit 1 row, purl 1 row*) until piece measures 1¾ (2, 2, 2¼, 2½) inches. Now increase 1 stitch at each side of next 6 rows—*30 (30, 32, 32, 34) stitches.* Then cast on 19 (20, 21, 22, 23) stitches at end of next 2 rows—*68 (70, 74, 76, 80) stitches.* Continue working in stockinette stitch, decreasing 1 stitch at each side every inch 3 times—*62 (64, 68, 70, 74) stitches.* Then work even in stockinette stitch until side edges of piece measure 7 (7½, 7¾, 8¼, 8½) inches, finishing with a purl row.

Waistband: Next Row (right side): Change to No. 3 needles and work even in knit 1, purl 1 ribbing for ¾ inch. Bind off in ribbing from wrong side of work.

BACK: Beginning at lower edge of crotch, with pink and No. 4 needles, cast on 18 (18, 20, 20, 22) stitches.

Work in stockinette stitch, increasing 1 stitch at each side of first 25 (26, 27, 28, 29) rows—*68 (70, 74, 76, 80) stitches.* Then decrease 1 stitch at each side every inch 3 times—*62 (64, 68, 70, 74) stitches.* Work even until side edges measure same length as side edges of front to lower edge of waistband, finishing with a purl row.

Shape Back (Short Rows): Row 1: Knit first 57 (59, 63, 65, 69) stitches, turn (*do not work last 5 stitches of row*).

Row 2: Slip first stitch, purl next 51 (53, 57, 59, 63) stitches, turn (*do not work last 5 stitches of row*).

Row 3: Slip first stitch, knit next 46 (48, 52, 54, 58) stitches, turn (*do not work last 10 stitches of row*).

Row 4: Slip first stitch, purl next 41 (43, 47, 49, 53) stitches, turn (*do not work last 10 stitches of row*).

Row 5: Slip first stitch, knit next 36 (38, 42, 44, 48) stitches, turn (*do not work last 15 stitches of row*).

Row 6: Slip first stitch, purl next 31 (33, 37, 39, 43) stitches, turn (*do not work last 15 stitches of row*).

Row 7: Slip first stitch, knit to end of row, working each slipped stitch together with stitch directly below it.

Row 8: Purl across entire row, working each remaining slipped stitch together with stitch directly below it—*62 (64, 68, 70, 74) stitches.*

Waistband: Next Row (right side): Change to No. 3 needles and work in knit 1, purl 1 ribbing for ¾ inch. Bind off in ribbing from wrong side of work.

FINISHING: Weave all remaining yarn ends into back of work. Block pieces lightly if necessary. Working from wrong side, seam front and back sections together at crotch.

LEG RIBBING: Working from right side of garment, with pink and No. 3 needles, pick up 63 (65, 67, 69, 71) stitches around edge of one leg. Work even in knit 1, purl 1 ribbing for ¾ inch. Bind off in ribbing from wrong side of work. Repeat around edge of other leg.

Sew side seams, working from wrong side. Then cut elastic to fit, stitch the ends together, and sew to inside of waistband.

Short-Sleeved Sweater, Romper and Bootees

SIZES: Directions are for size 4–8 months. Changes for size 8–12 months are given in parentheses. Sweater measures approximately 19½ (20¼) inches around chest.

MATERIALS: Baby or fingering yarn, 9 ounces purple, 2 ounces white. Knitting needles Nos. 2 and 4 (or size needed to obtain gauge). Crochet hook size B. Two stitch holders. Large-eyed tapestry needle. Five buttons.

GAUGE: 7 stitches = 1 inch; 9 rows = 1 inch (stockinette stitch, No. 4 needles).

SWEATER

BACK: Beginning at lower edge, with purple and No. 2 needles, cast on 70 (74) stitches. Work even in knit 1, purl 1 ribbing for 4 rows. Change to stockinette stitch (*knit 1 row, purl 1 row*) and work stripe pattern as follows: 4 rows white, 4 rows purple and 4 rows white. Then change to purple and No. 4 needles and work in stockinette stitch until piece measures 6½ (7½) inches or desired length to underarm, finishing with a purl row.

Shape Armholes: Continuing in stockinette stitch, bind off 4 stitches at beginning of next 2 rows, 2 stitches at beginning of next 2 rows and 1 stitch at beginning of next 4 rows—*54 (58) stitches.*

Divide for Center Back Opening: Next Row (right side): Knit first 27 (29) stitches; drop yarn without cutting it and attach another strand of purple; with new strand, knit remaining 27 (29) stitches. Working both sides at same time with separate strands of yarn, continue in stockinette stitch, except work the 2 stitches on each side of center back opening in garter stitch (*knit on all rows*). Work even in this manner until armholes measure 4 (4¼) inches, finishing with a purl row—*27 (29) stitches each side.*

Shape Neck and Shoulders: Working both sides at same time with separate strands of yarn, at each neck edge bind off 9 (10) stitches once, 2 stitches once and 1 stitch once; at same time, at each armhole edge bind off 5 (6) stitches once and 5 stitches twice.

FRONT: Work as for back to underarm.
Shape Armholes: Continuing in stockinette stitch, bind off 5 stitches at beginning of next 2 rows, 2 stitches at beginning of next 2 rows and 1 stitch at beginning of next 6 rows—*50 (54) stitches.* Work even in stockinette stitch until armholes measure 2 (2¼) inches, finishing with a purl row.
Shape Neck: Next Row (right side): Knit first 20 (21) stitches; drop yarn without cutting it and attach another

strand of purple; with new strand, bind off next 10 (12) stitches, knit to end of row—*20 (21) stitches each side.* Working both sides at same time with separate strands of yarn, at each neck edge bind off 2 stitches once and 1 stitch 3 times—*15 (16) stitches each side.* Then work even until armholes measure 4 (4¼) inches, finishing with a purl row.
Shape Shoulders: Working both sides at same time with separate strands of yarn, at each armhole edge bind off 5 (6) stitches once and 5 stitches twice.

RIGHT SLEEVE: Beginning at lower edge, with purple and No. 2 needles, cast on 44 (46) stitches. Work even in knit 1, purl 1 ribbing for 4 rows. Continuing in ribbing pattern as established, work 4 rows white, 4 rows purple and 4 rows white, increasing 1 stitch at each side on first row of each color—*50 (52) stitches.* After completing second white stripe, change to purple and No. 3 needles and work in stockinette stitch for 2 rows, finishing with a purl row.
Shape Cap: Continuing in stockinette stitch, bind off 5 stitches at beginning of next row (*front edge*), 3 stitches at beginning of next row (*back edge*), and 2 stitches at beginning of next 2 rows—*38 (40) stitches.* Now decrease 1 stitch at beginning of each row 14 (16) times—*24 stitches.* Then bind off 2 stitches at beginning of next 4 rows and 3 stitches at beginning of next 2 rows—*10 stitches.* Bind off remaining stitches.

LEFT SLEEVE: Work as for right sleeve to underarm.
Shape Cap: Continuing in stockinette stitch, bind off 3 stitches at beginning of next row (*back edge*), 5 stitches at beginning of next row (*front edge*), and 2 stitches at beginning of next 2 rows—*38 (40) stitches.* Now decrease 1 stitch at beginning of each row 14 (16) times—*24 stitches.* Then bind off 2 stitches at beginning of next 4 rows and 3 stitches at beginning of next 2 rows—*10 stitches.* Bind off remaining stitches.

FINISHING: Weave all remaining yarn ends into back of work. Block pieces lightly if necessary. Working from wrong side, seam front and back sections together at shoulders, sew sleeves to body, and then sew side and sleeve underarm seams.

NECKBAND: Working from right side of garment, with purple and No. 2 needles, pick up 71 (75) stitches around neck edge. Working even in knit 1, purl 1 ribbing, work 3 rows purple, 3 rows white and 3 rows purple. Bind off in ribbing.

With purple yarn, sew three buttonhole loops evenly spaced along one edge of center back opening. Sew buttons in position on opposite edge.

ROMPER

BACK: Beginning at lower edge of crotch, with purple and No. 4 needles, cast on 20 stitches. Work in stockinette stitch (*knit 1 row, purl 1 row*), increasing 1 stitch at each side of first 27 (28) rows—*74 (76) stitches.* Now decrease 1 stitch at each side every inch 3 times, working the decreases on the knit rows—*68 (70) stitches.* Work even for 2 inches, finishing with a purl row, and then increase 1 stitch at each side on next row—*70 (72) stitches.* Work even for 1 inch, finishing with a purl row, and then increase 1 stitch at each side on next row—*72 (74) stitches.* Now work even until piece measures 10 (11) inches from lower edge of crotch or desired length to underarm, finishing with a purl row.
Shape Armholes: Continuing in stockinette stitch, bind off 5 stitches at beginning of next 2 rows, 2 stitches at beginning of next 4 rows and 1 stitch at beginning of next 6 rows—*48 (50) stitches.*
Shape Neck: Next Row (right side): Knit first 17 stitches; drop yarn without cutting it and attach another strand of purple; with new strand, bind off next 14 (16) stitches, knit to end of row—*17 stitches each side.* Working both sides at same time with separate strands of yarn, at each neck edge bind off 3 stitches once, 2 stitches once and 1 stitch 4 times—*8 stitches each side.* Work even on each side until armholes measure 4½ (5) inches. Then bind off 2 stitches at each neck edge twice; and at the same time bind off 2 stitches at each armhole edge twice.

FRONT: Beginning at lower edge of crotch, with purple and No. 4 needles, cast on 20 stitches. Work even in stockinette stitch for 2 (2¼) inches, finishing with a purl row. Increase 1 stitch at each side of next 6 rows—*32 stitches.* Then cast on 21 (22) stitches at end of next 2 rows—*74 (76) stitches.* Work in stockinette stitch on all 74 (76) stitches for 4 rows, finishing with a purl row.
Divide for Center Front Insert: Next Row (right side): Knit first 30 (31) stitches; drop yarn without cutting it and attach another strand of purple; with new strand, bind off next 14 stitches, knit to end of row—*30 (31) stitches each side.* Working both sides at same time with separate strands of yarn, decrease 1 stitch at each side edge every inch 3 times, working the decreases on the knit rows—*27 (28) stitches each side.* Work even on both sides for 2 inches, finishing with a purl row, and then increase 1 stitch at each side edge on next row—*28 (29) stitches each side.* Work even on both sides for 1 inch, finishing with a purl row, and then increase 1 stitch at each side edge on next row—*29 (30) stitches each side.* Now work even on both sides until side edges measure same length as side edges of back to underarm, finishing with a purl row.
Shape Armholes: Working both sides at same time with separate strands of yarn, at each side edge bind off 5 stitches once, 2 stitches twice and 1 stitch 3 times—*17 (18) stitches each side.*
Shape Neck: Continuing to work both sides at same time with separate strands of yarn, at each neck edge bind off 4 stitches once, 2 stitches once and 1 stitch 3 (4) times—*8 stitches each side.* Then work even on both sides until armholes measure 4½ (5) inches, finishing with a purl row.
Next Row (Buttonhole Row): Knit 3, bind off next 2 stitches, knit to end of row, drop yarn; pick up yarn for second side and knit 3, bind off next 2 stitches, knit to end of row.
Next Row: Purl 3, cast on 2 stitches directly over bound-off stitches, purl 3, drop yarn; pick up yarn for other side and purl 3, cast on 2 stitches directly over bound-off stitches, purl 3—*8 stitches each side.* Then, working both sides at same time with separate strands of yarn, bind off 2 stitches at each neck edge twice, and at same time bind off 2 stitches at each side edge twice.

CENTER FRONT INSERT: With purple and No. 4 needles, cast on 60 (66) stitches. Purl 1 row. Then change to stockinette stitch and work stripe pattern as follows: 4 rows white, 4 rows purple, 4 rows white, 4 rows purple, 4 rows white and 1 row purple. Bind off all stitches.

FINISHING: Weave all remaining yarn ends into back of work. Block pieces lightly if necessary. Arrange center front insert in opening of front section, pin to hold, and sew in place from wrong side. Then seam front and back sections together at crotch.

LEG RIBBING: Working from right side of garment, with white and No. 2 needles, pick up 71 (75) stitches around edge of one leg. Then work even in knit 1, purl 1 ribbing as follows: 3 rows white and 3 rows purple. Bind off in ribbing. Repeat around edge of other leg. Now sew side seams, working from wrong side of garment.

ARMHOLE BANDS: Working from wrong side of garment, with white and No. 2 needles, pick up 104 (110) stitches around edge of one armhole, including top edges of front and back shoulder straps. Work even in stockinette stitch for 4 rows, working the purl rows on the *right* side of the garment and the knit rows on the *wrong* side. Bind off. Repeat around edge of other armhole.

NECKLINE BANDS: Working from wrong side of garment, pick up 90 (96) stitches around front neck edge. (*NOTE: Pick up these stitches only along garment edge, not along edges of armhole bands.*) Then work even in stockinette stitch for 4 rows, working the purl rows on the *right* side of the garment and the knit rows on the *wrong* side. Bind off. Repeat around back neck edge. Seam together ends of neckline and armhole bands at corners of shoulder straps. Sew buttons in position on back shoulder straps.

BOOTEES

Beginning at upper edge of cuff, with purple and No. 2 needles, loosely cast on 36 (38) stitches. Work even in knit 1, purl 1 ribbing for 4 rows. Change to No. 4 needles and stockinette stitch (*knit 1 row, purl 1 row*) and work in stripe pattern as follows: 4 rows white, 4 rows purple and 4 rows white. Then cut white, attach purple and work in stockinette stitch for 2 rows, finishing with a purl row.
Next Row (Eyelet Row): Continuing with purple for remainder of piece, * knit 1, yarn over, knit 2 together; repeat from * across row. Work next 5 rows in stockinette stitch, finishing with a purl row. Cut yarn.
Divide for Foot: Next Row (right side): Slip first 11 stitches onto a stitch holder for one side of foot; reattach purple and knit next 14 (16) stitches; slip remaining 11 stitches onto a stitch holder for other side of foot.

Shape Instep: Continuing in stockinette stitch, work center 14 (16) stitches until instep flap measures 2¼ (2½) inches. Bind off.

Shape Sides and Sole: Working from right side of piece, with purple and No. 2 needles, knit the 11 stitches from first stitch holder, pick up 16 (18) stitches along side of instep flap, place a marker on needle, pick up 14 stitches along front edge of instep flap, place a marker on needle, pick up 16 (18) stitches along other side of instep flap, knit the 11 stitches from second stitch holder—*68 (72) stitches.* Then work even in garter stitch (*knit each row*) for 9 (11) rows. (*NOTE: Keep markers in place on needle while working these rows.*)

Next Row (right side): Knit 2 together, knit to first marker, slip marker, knit 2 together, knit to 2 stitches before second marker, knit 2 together, slip marker, knit to last 2 stitches, knit last 2 stitches together—*64 (68) stitches.* Work next row even in garter stitch. Repeat these 2 rows twice—*56 (60) stitches.* Then work even in garter stitch for 4 rows. Bind off loosely.

Make second bootee in same manner

FINISHING: Weave all remaining yarn ends into back of work. Sew center back and sole seams, working from wrong side of piece. Make drawstrings for the bootees by crocheting two 15-inch chains, using doubled strands of purple yarn. Lace a drawstring through the eyelets of each bootee.

Overalls and Ribbed Pullover

SIZES: Directions are for size 1 year. Changes for sizes 2 and 3 years are given in parentheses. Overalls measure approximately 9¾ (11¾, 13¾) inches along inseam of leg. Pullover measures approximately 21½ (22½, 23½) inches around chest.

MATERIALS: Baby or fingering yarn, 7 (7, 9) ounces yellow, 6 (7, 7) ounces garnet red, 2 ounces orange. Knitting needles Nos. 2 and 3 (or size needed to obtain gauge). Crochet hook size C. One stitch holder. Large-eyed tapestry needle. One-half yard ¾-inch-wide elastic. Four snap fasteners. Three small buttons.

GAUGE: 15 stitches = 2 inches; 10 rows = 1 inch (stockinette stitch, No. 3 needles).

OVERALLS

LEFT LEG: Beginning at lower edge, with red and No. 3 needles, cast on 59 (64, 69) stitches, place a marker on needle, cast on 59 (64, 69) stitches—*118 (128, 138) stitches.* Working in garter stitch (*knit each row*), work 28 rows with red, 28 rows with orange and 28 rows with yellow. At same time, decrease 4 stitches on seventh row of red stripe in the following way: knit 2 together, knit to 3 stitches before marker, knit 2 together, knit 1, slip marker, knit 1, knit 2 together, knit to last 2 stitches, knit last 2 stitches together—*114 (124, 134) stitches.* Repeat this decrease row every 8 rows 7 (8, 9) times—*86 (92, 98) stitches.* Continue working even in garter stitch until yellow stripe has been completed. Then cut yellow, attach red and work even in stockinette stitch (*knit 1 row, purl 1 row*) until piece measures 6½ (8½, 10½) inches, finishing with a purl row. Now increase 1 stitch at each side every 4 rows 7 times—*100 (106, 112) stitches.* Work even until piece measures 9¾ (11¾, 13¾) inches, finishing with a purl row.
Shape Crotch: Next Row (right side): Continuing in stockinette stitch, bind off first 3 stitches (*center back edge*), knit remaining stitches of row—*97 (103, 109) stitches.* Mark center back edge by inserting a safety pin in first bound-off stitch.
Next Row (wrong side): Bind off first 2 stitches (*center front edge*), purl remaining stitches of row—*95 (101, 107) stitches.*
Next Row: Bind off first 2 stitches (*center back edge*), knit remaining stitches of row—*93 (99, 105) stitches.*
Next Row: Bind off first 2 stitches (*center front edge*), purl remaining stitches of row—*91 (97, 103) stitches.*
Next Row: Knit first 2 stitches together (*center back edge*), knit remaining stitches of row—*90 (96, 102) stitches.*
Next Row: Purl even across row.
Next Row: Knit first 2 stitches together (*center back edge*),

knit remaining stitches of row—*89 (95, 101) stitches.* Work next 9 rows even in stockinette stitch. Repeat these 10 rows 3 times—*86 (92, 98) stitches.* Then work even in stockinette stitch until piece measures 7½ (7¾, 8¼) inches from first bound-off row of crotch, finishing with a purl row.
Shape Back (Short Rows): Row 1: Starting at center back edge, knit first 37 stitches, turn (*do not work remaining stitches of row*).
Row 2: Slip first stitch, purl 36.
Row 3: Knit first 31 stitches, turn (*do not work remaining stitches of row*).
Row 4: Slip first stitch, purl 30.
Row 5: Knit first 25 stitches, turn (*do not work remaining stitches of row*).
Row 6: Slip first stitch, purl 24.
Row 7: Knit across entire row, working each slipped stitch together with stitch directly below it—*86 (92, 98) stitches.*
Row 8: Purl even across row.
Waistband: Next Row (right side): Change to No. 2 needles and, starting at center back edge, work first 43 (46, 49) stitches of row in knit 1, purl 1 ribbing; insert a safety pin into next stitch to mark side edge of bib, and slip this stitch and remaining 42 (45, 48) stitches onto a stitch holder for bib. Work stitches on needle in knit 1, purl 1 ribbing as established for 1 inch. Bind off in ribbing from wrong side of piece.
Bib: Slip the 43 (46, 49) stitches from stitch holder onto a No. 3 needle, retaining safety pin marker. Reattach red at marked stitch and work in stockinette stitch with No. 3 needles for 1 inch, starting with a knit row and finishing with a purl row. Now change to garter stitch and work in stripes of 2 rows red, 2 rows orange and 2 rows yellow, repeating these 6 rows for pattern. At same time, at side edge of bib bind off 10 (11, 12) stitches once, 3 stitches once, 2 stitches once and 1 stitch 7 times—*21 (23, 25) stitches.* Then work even in stripe pattern until 12 (12, 13) stripes of each color have been completed. Bind off.

RIGHT LEG: Work as for left leg to shaping of crotch.
Shape Crotch: Next Row (right side): Bind off first 2 stitches (*center front edge*), knit remaining stitches of row—*98 (104, 110) stitches.*
Next Row (wrong side): Bind off first 3 stitches (*center back edge*), mark center back edge by inserting a safety pin in first bound-off stitch of row, purl remaining stitches of row—*95 (101, 107) stitches.*
Next Row: Bind off first 2 stitches (*center front edge*), knit remaining stitches of row—*93 (99, 105) stitches.*
Next Row: Bind off first 2 stitches (*center back edge*), purl remaining stitches of row—*91 (97, 103) stitches.*

Overalls and Ribbed Pullover

Next Row: Knit to last 2 stitches, knit last 2 stitches together (*center back edge*)—90 (96, 102) stitches.
Next Row: Purl even across row.
Next Row: Knit to last 2 stitches, knit last 2 stitches together (*center back edge*)—89 (95, 101) stitches. Work next 9 rows even in stockinette stitch. Repeat these 10 rows 3 times—86 (92, 98) stitches. Then work even in stockinette stitch until piece measures 7½, (7¾, 8¼) inches from first bound-off row of crotch, finishing with a knit row.
Shape Back (Short Rows): Row 1: Starting at center back edge, purl first 37 stitches, turn (*do not work remaining stitches of row*).
Row 2: Slip first stitch, knit 36.
Row 3: Purl first 31 stitches, turn (*do not work remaining stitches of row*).
Row 4: Slip first stitch, knit 30.
Row 5: Purl first 25 stitches, turn (*do not work remaining stitches of row*).
Row 6: Slip first stitch, knit 24.
Row 7: Purl across entire row, working each slipped stitch together with stitch directly below it—86 (92, 98) stitches.
Row 8: Knit even across row.
Waistband: Next Row (wrong side): Change to No. 2 needles and, starting at center back edge, work first 43 (46, 49) stitches of row in knit 1, purl 1 ribbing; insert a safety pin into next stitch to mark side edge of bib, and slip this stitch and remaining 42 (45, 48) stitches onto a stitch holder for bib. Work stitches on needle in knit 1, purl 1 ribbing as established for 1 inch. Bind off in ribbing from wrong side of piece.
Bib: Slip the 43 (46, 49) stitches from stitch holder onto a No. 3 needle, retaining safety pin marker. Reattach red at marked stitch and work in stockinette stitch with No. 3 needles for 1 inch, starting with a purl row and finishing with a knit row. Now change to garter stitch and work in stripes of 2 rows red, 2 rows orange and 2 rows yellow, repeating these 6 rows for pattern. At same time, at side edge of bib bind off 10 (11, 12) stitches once, 3 stitches once, 2 stitches once and 1 stitch 7 times—21 (23, 25) stitches. Then work even in stripe pattern until 12 (12, 13) stripes of each color have been completed. Bind off.

SHOULDER STRAPS: (Make 2.) With red and No. 2 needles, cast on 8 stitches. Work even in garter stitch for 13½ (15½, 17½) inches or desired length. Bind off.

FINISHING: Weave all remaining yarn ends into back of work. Block pieces lightly if necessary. Working from wrong side, sew inseam of each leg. Then stitch the legs together from wrong side, carefully matching waistband edges and intersection of inseams, as well as stripes and top edge of bib. Cut elastic to fit and sew to inside of waistband. Stitch ends of waistband to side edges of bib. Now, with red and size C crochet hook, work 2 rows of single crochet stitches around edges of bib, working first row from right side and second row from wrong side. Finally, stitch one end of each shoulder strap to waistband, and sew two snap fasteners in position along the other end of each strap and just inside the top edge of the bib at the corners.

PULLOVER

BACK: Beginning at lower edge, with yellow and No. 2 needles, cast on 82 (86, 90) stitches. Work even in knit 2, purl 2 ribbing for 1 inch. Then change to No. 3 needles and continue working even in ribbing pattern as established until piece measures 8 (9, 10) inches or desired length to underarm, working last row on wrong side.
Shape Raglan Armholes: Continuing in ribbing pattern as established, bind off 3 stitches at beginning of next 2 rows—76 (80, 84) stitches. Then decrease 1 stitch at each side every other row 24 (26, 28) times, working the decreases on the right side of the piece—28 stitches. Bind off.

FRONT: Work as for back to underarm.
Shape Raglan Armholes: Continuing in ribbing pattern as established, bind off 3 stitches at beginning of next 2 rows—76 (80, 84) stitches. Then decrease 1 stitch at each side every other row 13 (15, 16) times, working the decreases on the right side of the piece—50 (50, 52) stitches. Work next row even on wrong side of piece.
Shape Neck: Next Row (right side): Continuing in ribbing pattern, work first 2 stitches together, work next 17 (17, 18) stitches; drop yarn without cutting it and attach another strand of yellow; with new strand, bind off next 12 stitches, work in ribbing pattern to last 2 stitches, work last 2 stitches together—18 (18, 19) stitches each side. Working both sides at same time with separate strands of yarn, at each neck edge bind off 3 stitches once, 2 stitches once and 1 stitch 5 times; at same time, continue to decrease 1 stitch at each armhole edge every other row as before until only 2 stitches remain on each side. Bind off remaining stitches on each side.

RIGHT SLEEVE: Beginning at lower edge, with yellow and No. 2 needles, cast on 38 (42, 46) stitches. Work even in knit 2, purl 2 ribbing for 1 inch. Change to No. 3 needles and continue working in ribbing pattern as established, increasing 1 stitch at each side every 4 rows 12 times—62 (66, 70) stitches. Then work even until piece measures 8 (9, 10) inches or desired length to underarm, working last row on wrong side.
Shape Raglan Cap: Continuing in ribbing pattern as established, bind off 3 stitches at beginning of next 2 rows—56 (60, 64) stitches. Then decrease 1 stitch at each side every other row 22 (24, 26) times, working the decreases on the right side of the piece—12 stitches.
Next Row (wrong side): Work even in ribbing pattern across row.
Next Row (right side): Bind off first 3 stitches (*front edge*), work in ribbing pattern to last 2 stitches, work last 2 stitches together—8 stitches.
Next Row: Work in ribbing pattern across row.
Next Row: Bind off first 3 stitches (*front edge*), work in ribbing pattern to last 2 stitches, work last 2 stitches together—4 stitches.
Next Row: Work even in ribbing pattern across row. Bind off.

LEFT SLEEVE: Work as for right sleeve to underarm.
Shape Raglan Cap: Continuing in ribbing pattern as established, bind off 3 stitches at beginning of next 2 rows—56 (60, 64) stitches. Then decrease 1 stitch at each side every other row 22 (24, 26) times, working the decreases on the right side of the piece—12 stitches.
Next Row (wrong side): Bind off first 3 stitches (*front edge*), work remaining 8 stitches in ribbing pattern—9 stitches.
Next Row (right side): Work first 2 stitches together,

work remaining 7 stitches in ribbing pattern—*8 stitches*.
Next Row: Bind off first 3 stitches (*front edge*), work remaining 4 stitches in ribbing pattern—*5 stitches*.
Next Row: Work first 2 stitches together, work remaining 3 stitches in ribbing pattern—*4 stitches*. Bind off.

FINISHING: Weave all remaining yarn ends into back of work. Block pieces lightly if necessary. Working from wrong side, sew sleeves to front and back sections, leaving approximately 3 inches open at neck edge of left back raglan seam. Then sew side and sleeve underarm seams.

NECKBAND: Working from right side of garment, with yellow and No. 2 needles, pick up 82 (84, 86) stitches around neck edge, starting and ending at open portion of left back raglan seam. Work even in knit 2, purl 2 ribbing for 1 inch. Bind off in ribbing from wrong side of work.

Sew three yarn loops evenly spaced along one edge of left back opening. Sew buttons in position along opposite edge of opening.

Cable Cardigan and Peaked Cap

SIZES: Directions are for size 6 months. Changes for sizes 1, 2 and 3 years are given in parentheses. Cardigan measures approximately 20¼ (21½, 22½, 23¾) inches around chest.

MATERIALS: Baby or fingering yarn, 6 (7, 7, 9) ounces white. Knitting needles Nos. 2 and 3 (or size needed to obtain gauge). Crochet hook size B. One cable holder or No. 3 double-pointed needle. Large-eyed tapestry needle. Six buttons.

GAUGE: 15 stitches = 2 inches; 10 rows = 1 inch (stockinette stitch, No. 3 needles).

CABLE PATTERN: Work as follows over each group of 10 stitches indicated in directions for making cardigan:

Row 1 (right side): Purl 2, knit 6, purl 2.
Row 2 (wrong side): Knit 2, purl 6, knit 2.
Row 3: Purl 2, knit 6, purl 2.
Row 4: Knit 2, purl 6, knit 2.
Row 5 (Cable Row): Purl 2, slip next 3 stitches onto cable holder and hold in back of work, knit next 3 stitches, then knit the 3 stitches from cable holder, purl 2.
Row 6: Knit 2, purl 6, knit 2.
Row 7: Purl 2, knit 6, purl 2.
Row 8: Knit 2, purl 6, knit 2. Repeat Rows 1–8 for cable pattern.

CARDIGAN

BACK: Beginning at lower edge, with No. 2 needles, cast on 80 (86, 90, 96) stitches. Work even in knit 1, purl 1 ribbing for 1 inch.
Next Row (right side): Change to No. 3 needles. Knit 16 (18, 19, 20), place a marker on needle, work Row 1 of cable pattern on next 10 stitches, place a marker on needle, knit next 28 (30, 32, 36) stitches, place a marker on needle, work Row 1 of cable pattern on next 10 stitches, place a marker on needle, knit remaining 16 (18, 19, 20) stitches.
Next Row (wrong side): Purl 16 (18, 19, 20), slip marker, work Row 2 of cable pattern on next 10 stitches, slip marker, purl 28 (30, 32, 36), slip marker, work Row 2 of cable pattern on next 10 stitches, slip marker, purl remaining 16 (18, 19, 20) stitches. Continue to work each group of 10 stitches between markers in cable pattern and remaining stitches in stockinette stitch (*knit 1 row, purl 1 row*) until piece measures 7 (7¾, 8½, 9¼) inches or desired length to underarm, working last row on wrong side.

Shape Raglan Armholes: Continuing in stockinette stitch and cable pattern as established, bind off 5 stitches at beginning of next 2 rows—*70 (76, 80, 86) stitches.* Then decrease 1 stitch at each side every other row 20 (22, 24, 26) times—*30 (32, 32, 34) stitches.* Bind off.

RIGHT FRONT: Beginning at lower edge, with No. 2 needles, cast on 38 (40, 43, 46) stitches. Work even in knit 1, purl 1 ribbing for 1 inch.
Next Row (right side): Change to No. 3 needles. Knit 12 (12, 14, 16), place a marker on needle, work Row 1 of cable pattern on next 10 stitches, place a marker on needle, knit remaining 16 (18, 19, 20) stitches.
Next Row (wrong side): Purl 16 (18, 19, 20), slip marker, work Row 2 of cable pattern on next 10 stitches, slip marker, purl remaining 12 (12, 14, 16) stitches. Continue to work the group of 10 stitches between markers in cable pattern and remaining stitches in stockinette stitch until piece measures same length as back to underarm, working last row on right side.
Shape Raglan Armhole: Continuing in stockinette stitch and cable pattern as established, bind off 5 stitches at beginning of next row (armhole edge)—*33 (35, 38, 41) stitches.* Then decrease 1 stitch at armhole edge every other row 12 (14, 15, 16) times, working the decreases on the right side of the piece—*21 (21, 23, 25) stitches.* Work next row even on wrong side.
Shape Neck: Continuing in stockinette stitch and cable pattern as established, at neck edge bind off 6 stitches once, 3 stitches once, 2 stitches once and 1 stitch 2 (2, 3, 4) times; at same time, continue to decrease 1 stitch at armhole edge every other row as before until only 2 stitches remain. Bind off.

LEFT FRONT: Beginning at lower edge, with No. 2 needles, cast on 38 (40, 43, 46) stitches. Work even in knit 1, purl 1 ribbing for 1 inch.
Next Row (right side): Change to No. 3 needles. Knit 16 (18, 19, 20), place a marker on needle, work Row 1 of cable pattern on next 10 stitches, place a marker on needle, knit remaining 12 (12, 14, 16) stitches.
Next Row (wrong side): Purl 12 (12, 14, 16), slip marker, work Row 2 of cable pattern on next 10 stitches, slip marker, purl remaining 16 (18, 19, 20) stitches. Continue to work the group of 10 stitches between markers in cable pattern and remaining stitches in stockinette stitch until piece measures same length as back to underarm, working last row on wrong side.
Shape Raglan Armhole: Continuing in stockinette stitch and cable pattern as established, bind off 5 stitches at beginning of next row (armhole edge)—*33 (35, 38, 41) stitches.* Then decrease 1 stitch at armhole edge every

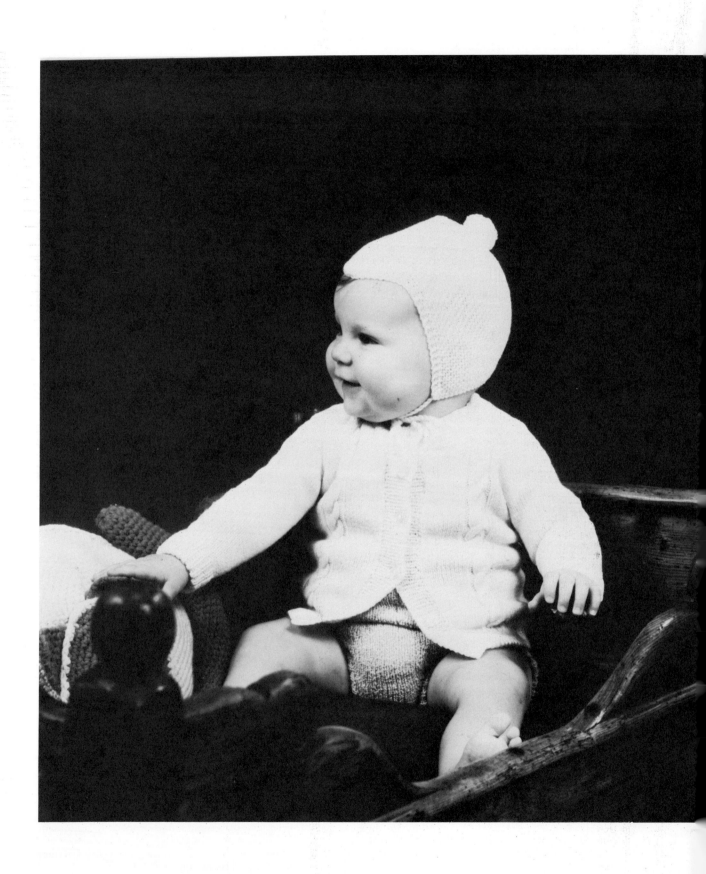

other row 12 (14, 15, 16) times, working the decreases on the right side of the piece—*21 (21, 23, 25) stitches.*

Shape Neck: Continuing in stockinette stitch and cable pattern as established, at neck edge bind off 6 stitches once, 3 stitches once, 2 stitches once and 1 stitch 2 (2, 3, 4) times; at same time, continue to decrease 1 stitch at armhole edge every other row as before until only 2 stitches remain. Bind off.

RIGHT SLEEVE: Beginning at lower edge, with No. 2 needles, cast on 42 (44, 46, 48) stitches. Work even in knit 1, purl 1 ribbing for 2 inches.

Next Row (right side): Change to No. 3 needles. Knit 16 (17, 18, 19), place a marker on needle, work Row 1 of cable pattern on next 10 stitches, place a marker on needle, knit remaining 16 (17, 18, 19) stitches.

Next Row (wrong side): Purl 16 (17, 18, 19), slip marker, work Row 2 of cable pattern on next 10 stitches, slip marker, purl remaining 16 (17, 18, 19) stitches. Continue to work the group of 10 stitches between markers in cable pattern and remaining stitches in stockinette stitch, and at same time increase 1 stitch at each side every 4 rows 9 (10, 11, 12) times—*60 (64, 68, 72) stitches.* Then work even in stockinette stitch and cable pattern as established until piece measures 7¾ (8½, 9¼, 10) inches or desired length to underarm, working last row on wrong side.

Shape Raglan Cap: Continuing in stockinette stitch and cable pattern as established, bind off 5 stitches at beginning of next 2 rows—*50 (54, 58, 62) stitches.* Then decrease 1 stitch at each side every other row 18 (20, 22, 24) times, working the decreases on the knit rows—*14 stitches.*

Next Row (wrong side): Purl 2, knit 2, purl 6, knit 2, purl 2.

Next Row (right side): Bind off first 3 stitches (*front edge*), knit 6, purl 2, knit last 2 stitches together—*10 stitches.*

Next Row: Purl 1, knit 2, purl 6, knit 1.

Next Row: Bind off first 3 stitches (*front edge*), knit 3, purl 1, purl last 2 stitches together—*6 stitches.*

Next Row: Knit 2, purl 4.

Next Row: Bind off first 3 stitches (*front edge*), purl 2—*3 stitches.*

Next Row: Purl 2, knit 1. Bind off.

LEFT SLEEVE: Work as for right sleeve to underarm.

Shape Raglan Cap: Continuing in stockinette stitch and cable pattern as established, bind off 5 stitches at beginning of next 2 rows—*50 (54, 58, 62) stitches.* Then decrease 1 stitch at each side every other row 18 (20, 22, 24) times, working the decreases on the knit rows—*14 stitches.*

Next Row (wrong side): Bind off first 3 stitches (*front edge*), purl 6, knit 2, purl 2—*11 stitches.*

Next Row (right side): Knit first 2 stitches together, purl 2, knit 6, purl 1—*10 stitches.*

Next Row: Bind off first 3 stitches (*front edge*), purl 3, knit 2, purl 1—*7 stitches.*

Next Row: Knit first 2 stitches together, purl 1, knit 4—*6 stitches.*

Next Row: Bind off first 3 stitches (*front edge*), knit 2—*3 stitches.*

Next Row: Purl 2, knit 1. Bind off.

FINISHING: Weave all remaining yarn ends into back of work. Block pieces lightly if necessary. Working from

wrong side, sew sleeves to front and back sections. Then sew side and sleeve underarm seams.

NECKBAND: Working from right side of garment, with No. 2 needles, pick up 83 (87, 91, 95) stitches around neck edge. Work even in knit 1, purl 1 ribbing for 1 inch. Bind off in ribbing from wrong side of work.

LEFT FRONT BAND: Working from right side of garment, with No. 1 needles, pick up stitches evenly along left front edge. Work even in knit 1, purl 1 ribbing for 1 inch. Bind off in ribbing from wrong side of work.

RIGHT FRONT BAND: Work as for left front band until ribbing measures ½ inch. With pins, mark position of six buttonholes evenly spaced along front edge, inserting top pin ¾ inch from neck edge and bottom pin ¾ inch from lower edge.

Next Row (Buttonhole Row): * Work in ribbing pattern as established to 1 stitch before pin marker, bind off next 2 stitches; repeat from * 5 times; work in ribbing to end of row.

Next Row: * Work in ribbing pattern as established to bound-off stitches, cast on 2 stitches directly over bound-off stitches; repeat from * 5 times; work in ribbing to end of row. Then work even in ribbing until band measures 1 inch. Bind off in ribbing from wrong side of work.

Sew buttons in position on left front band.

(*NOTE: For a boy's sweater, make buttonholes on left front band instead of on right front band.*)

PEAKED CAP

With No. 3 needles, cast on 36 (38, 40, 42) stitches. Work in garter stitch (*knit each row*) as follows:

Row 1: Knit even across row.

Next Row: Knit 2, knit 2 together (*1 decrease made*), knit to last 3 stitches, knit in front and in back of next stitch (*1 increase made*), knit 2. Knit even across next row. Repeat these 2 rows 18 (20, 22, 24) times.

Next Row: Knit 2, knit in front and in back of next stitch (*1 increase made*), knit to last 4 stitches, knit 2 together (*1 decrease made*), knit 2. Knit even across next row. Repeat these 2 rows 18 (20, 22, 24) times.

Next Row: Knit 2, knit 2 together (*1 decrease made*), knit to last 3 stitches, knit in front and in back of next stitch (*1 increase made*), knit 2. Knit even across next row. Repeat these 2 rows 8 (10, 12, 14) times.

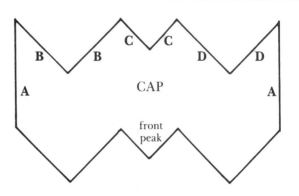

ASSEMBLING THE CAP. Sew together corresponding edges (indicated by the same letter).

Next Row: Knit 2, knit in front and in back of next stitch (*1 increase made*), knit to last 4 stitches, knit 2 together (*1 decrease made*), knit 2. Knit even across next row. Repeat these 2 rows 8 (10, 12, 14) times.

Next Row: Knit 2, knit 2 together (*1 decrease made*), knit to last 3 stitches, knit in front and in back of next stitch (*1 increase made*), knit 2. Knit even across next row. Repeat these 2 rows 18 (20, 22, 24) times.

Next Row: Knit 2, knit in front and in back of next stitch (*1 increase made*), knit to last 4 stitches, knit 2 together (*1 decrease made*), knit 2. Knit even across next row. Repeat these 2 rows 18 (20, 22, 24) times. Bind off all stitches.

FINISHING: Weave all remaining yarn ends into back of work. Working from wrong side, seam back and side edges together (*see diagram*). Make ties for the cap by crocheting two 15-inch chains, using doubled strands of yarn. Sew ties to cap at sides. Make a small pompon and sew to top of cap.

Short-Sleeved Polo Shirt, Romper and Bootees

SIZES: Directions are for size 3 months. Changes for sizes 6, 9, 12 and 15 months are given in parentheses. Polo shirt measures approximately 18 (18¾, 19½, 21¼, 21½) inches around chest and 8½ (9½, 10½, 11½, 12½) inches from shoulder to bottom edge.

MATERIALS: Baby or fingering yarn, 6 (6, 7, 7, 7) ounces blue, 2 ounces white. Knitting needles Nos. 2 and 4 (or size needed to obtain gauge). Crochet hook size B. Two stitch holders. Large-eyed tapestry needle. Eight buttons.

GAUGE: 7 stitches = 1 inch; 9 rows = 1 inch (stockinette stitch, No. 4 needles).

STRIPE PATTERN: Working in stockinette stitch (*knit 1 row, purl 1 row*), work 2 rows white and 2 rows blue. Repeat these 4 rows for pattern, carrying color not in use at side of work.

POLO SHIRT

BACK: Beginning at lower edge, with blue and No. 2 needles, cast on 66 (68, 70, 74, 78) stitches.
Work even in knit 1, purl 1 ribbing for 1 inch. Change to No. 4 needles and work even in stripe pattern until piece measures 4½ (5½, 6¼, 7, 8) inches or desired length to underarm, finishing with a purl row.
Shape Raglan Armholes: Continuing in stripe pattern as established, bind off 3 stitches at beginning of next 2 rows—*60 (62, 64, 68, 72) stitches.* Then decrease 1 stitch at each side every other row 18 (19, 20, 21, 22) times, working the decreases on the knit rows—*24 (24, 24, 26, 28) stitches.* Bind off.

FRONT: Work as for back until piece measures 4 (4½, 5½, 6¼, 7) inches, finishing with a purl row.
Divide for Center Front Placket: Next Row (right side): Continuing in stripe pattern as established, knit first 30 (31, 32, 34, 36) stitches; drop yarn without cutting it and attach another strand of same color; with new strand, bind off next 6 stitches, knit to end of row—*30 (31, 32, 34, 36) stitches each side.* Working both sides at same time with separate strands of yarn, continue in stripe pattern until piece measures same length as back to underarm, finishing with a purl row in same color as on back at underarm.
Shape Raglan Armholes: Continuing to work in stripe pattern on both sides at same time, bind off 3 stitches at each armhole edge—*27 (28, 29, 31, 33) stitches each side.* Then decrease 1 stitch at each armhole edge every other row 11 (12, 13, 14, 15) times, working the decreases on the knit rows—*6 (6, 6, 7, 8) stitches each side.*

Shape Neck: Continuing to work in stripe pattern on both sides at same time, at each neck edge bind off 4 (4, 4, 5, 6) stitches once, 2 stitches once and 1 stitch 3 times; at same time continue to decrease 1 stitch at each armhole edge every other row as before until only 2 stitches remain on each side. Bind off remaining stitches on each side.

RIGHT SLEEVE: Beginning at lower edge, with blue and No. 2 needles, cast on 41 (43, 45, 47, 49) stitches. Work even in knit 1, purl 1 ribbing for 4 rows. Change to No. 4 needles and work in stripe pattern, increasing 1 stitch at each side every other row 4 times—*49 (51, 53, 55, 57) stitches.* Then work even in stripe pattern until piece measures 1½ (1½, 1½, 2, 2) inches or desired length to underarm, finishing with a purl row in same color as on front and back at underarm.
Shape Raglan Cap: Continuing in stripe pattern, bind off 3 stitches at beginning of next 2 rows—*43 (45, 47, 49, 51) stitches.* Then decrease 1 stitch at each side every other row 16 (17, 18, 19, 20) times, working the decreases on the knit rows—*11 stitches.*
Next Row (wrong side): Purl even across row.
Next Row (right side): Bind off first 3 stitches (*front edge*), knit to last 2 stitches, knit last 2 stitches together—*7 stitches.*
Next Row: Purl even across row.
Next Row: Bind off first 3 stitches (*front edge*), knit to last 2 stitches, knit last 2 stitches together—*3 stitches.*
Next Row: Purl even across row. Bind off.

LEFT SLEEVE: Work as for right sleeve to underarm.
Shape Raglan Cap: Continuing in stripe pattern, bind off 3 stitches at beginning of next 2 rows—*43 (45, 47, 49, 51) stitches.* Then decrease 1 stitch at each side every other row 16 (17, 18, 19, 20) times, working the decreases on the knit rows—*11 stitches.*
Next Row (wrong side): Bind off first 3 stitches (*front edge*), purl remaining 7 stitches—*8 stitches.*
Next Row (right side): Knit first 2 stitches together, knit remaining 6 stitches—*7 stitches.*
Next Row: Bind off first 3 stitches (*front edge*), purl remaining 3 stitches—*4 stitches.*
Next Row: Knit first 2 stitches together, knit remaining 2 stitches—*3 stitches.*
Next Row: Purl even across row. Bind off.

FINISHING: Weave all remaining yarn ends into back of work. Block pieces lightly if necessary. Working from wrong side, sew sleeves to front and back sections. Then sew side and sleeve underarm seams.

NECKBAND: Working from right side of garment, with

blue and No. 2 needles, pick up 63 (65, 67, 69, 71) stitches around neck edge. Work even in knit 1, purl 1 ribbing for 8 rows. Bind off in ribbing from wrong side of work.

RIGHT FRONT PLACKET: Working from right side of garment, with blue and No. 2 needles, pick up stitches evenly along right front edge. Work even in knit 1, purl 1 ribbing for 8 rows. Bind off.

LEFT FRONT PLACKET: Work as for left front placket until 3 rows of ribbing have been completed. With pins, mark position of four buttonholes evenly spaced along front edge, inserting top pin ¾ inch from neck edge and bottom pin ¾ inch from lower edge of placket.
Next Row (Buttonhole Row): * Work in ribbing pattern as established to 1 stitch before pin marker, bind off next 2 stitches; repeat from * 3 times; work in ribbing to end of row.
Next Row: * Work in ribbing pattern as established to bound-off stitches, cast on 2 stitches directly over bound-off stitches; repeat from * 3 times; work in ribbing to end of row. Then work even in ribbing for 3 rows. Bind off.

Lap left front placket over right front placket, aligning lower edges, and sew lower edges to garment front. Sew buttons in position on right front placket.

(NOTE: For a girl's polo shirt, make buttonholes on right front placket instead of on left front placket, and lap right placket over left placket before stitching lower edges to garment.)

ROMPER

BACK: Beginning at lower edge of crotch, with blue and No. 4 needles, cast on 18 (18, 20, 20, 22) stitches. Work in stockinette stitch (*knit 1 row, purl 1 row*), increasing 1 stitch at each side of first 25 (26, 27, 28, 29) rows—*68 (70, 74, 76, 80) stitches*. Then decrease 1 stitch at each side every inch 3 times—*62 (64, 68, 70, 74) stitches*. Work even until side edges measure 6¼ (6½, 6½, 7, 7) inches, finishing with a purl row.
Shape Back (Short Rows): Row 1: Knit first 57 (59, 63, 65, 69) stitches turn (*do not work last 5 stitches of row*).
Row 2: Slip first stitch, purl next 51 (53, 57, 59, 63) stitches, turn (*do not work last 5 stitches of row*).
Row 3: Slip first stitch, knit next 46 (48, 52, 54, 58) stitches, turn (*do not work last 10 stitches of row*).
Row 4: Slip first stitch, purl next 41 (43, 47, 49, 53) stitches, turn (*do not work last 10 stitches of row*).
Row 5: Slip first stitch, knit next 36 (38, 42, 44, 48) stitches, turn (*do not work last 15 stitches of row*).
Row 6: Slip first stitch, purl next 31 (33, 37, 39, 43) stitches, turn (*do not work last 15 stitches of row*).
Row 7: Slip first stitch, knit across to end of row, working each slipped stitch together with stitch directly below it.
Row 8: Purl across entire row, working each remaining slipped stitch together with stitch directly below it—*62 (64, 68, 70, 74) stitches*. Then work even until side edges of piece measure 8¼ (9¼, 10¼, 10¾, 11¼) inches or desired length to underarm, finishing with a purl row.
Shape Armholes: Continuing in stockinette stitch, bind off 5 stitches at beginning of next 2 rows, 3 stitches at beginning of next 2 rows, 2 stitches at beginning of next 2 rows and 1 stitch at beginning of next 6 rows—*36 (38, 42, 44, 48) stitches*.
Shape Neck: Next Row (right side): Knit first 13 (13, 14, 14, 15) stitches; drop yarn without cutting it and

attach another strand of blue; with new strand, bind off next 10 (12, 14, 16, 18) stitches, knit to end of row—*13 (13, 14, 14, 15) stitches each side*. Working both sides at same time with separate strands of yarn, at each neck edge bind off 3 stitches once, 2 stitches once, and 1 stitch 5 times—*3 (3, 4, 4, 5) stitches each side*. Then work even on both sides until armholes measure 4¼ (4½, 4½, 4¾, 5) inches. Bind off remaining stitches on each side.

FRONT: Beginning at lower edge of crotch, with blue and No. 4 needles, cast on 18 (18, 20, 20, 22) stitches. Work even in stockinette stitch for 1¾ (2, 2, 2¼, 2½) inches, finishing with a purl row. Increase 1 stitch at each side of next 6 rows—*30 (30, 32, 32, 34) stitches*. Then cast on 19 (20, 21, 22, 23) stitches at end of next 2 rows—*68 (70, 74, 76, 80) stitches*. Continue working in stockinette stitch on all 68 (70, 74, 76, 80) stitches, decreasing 1 stitch at each side every inch 3 times—*62 (64, 68, 70, 74) stitches*. Work even until side edges of piece measure same length as side edges of back to underarms, finishing with a purl row.
Shape Armholes: Continuing in stockinette stitch, bind off 5 stitches at beginning of next 2 rows, 3 stitches at beginning of next 2 rows, 2 stitches at beginning of next 2 rows and 1 stitch at beginning of next 6 rows—*36 (38, 42, 44, 48) stitches*.
Shape Neck: Next Row (right side): Knit first 13 (13, 14, 14, 15) stitches; drop yarn without cutting it and attach another strand of blue, with new strand, bind off next 10 (12, 14, 16, 18) stitches, knit to end of row—*13 (13, 14, 14, 15) stitches each side*. Working both sides at same time with separate strands of yarn, at each neck edge bind off 3 stitches once, 2 stitches once and 1 stitch 5 times—*3 (3, 4, 4, 5) stitches each side*. Work even on both sides until armholes measure 4¼ (4½, 4½, 4¾, 5) inches. Bind off remaining stitches on each side.

FINISHING: Weave all remaining yarn ends into back of work. Block pieces lightly if necessary. Working from wrong side, seam front and back sections together at crotch.

LEG RIBBING: Working from right side of garment, with blue and No. 2 needles, pick up 63 (65, 67, 69, 73) stitches around edge of one leg. Work even in knit 1, purl 1 ribbing for ¾ inch. Bind off in ribbing from wrong side of work. Repeat around edge of other leg. Then sew side seams, working from wrong side of garment.

NECKLINE RIBBING: Working from right side of garment, with blue and No. 2 needles, pick up 65 (67, 69, 71, 73) stitches around front neck edge. Work even in knit 1, purl 1 ribbing for ½ inch. Bind off in ribbing from wrong side of work. Repeat around back neck edge.

ARMHOLE RIBBING: Working from right side of garment, with blue and No. 2 needles, pick up 75 (77, 79, 81, 83) stitches around edge of one armhole. Work even in knit 1, purl 1 ribbing for ½ inch. Bind off in ribbing from wrong side of work. Repeat around edge of other armhole.

SHOULDER EDGING: With blue and size B crochet hook, work 2 rows of single crochet stitches across end of each back shoulder strap. Repeat across end of each front shoulder strap; but this time, on second row, work two evenly spaced chain-stitch buttonhole loops on each strap. Then sew two buttons in position on each back shoulder strap.

BOOTEES

Beginning at upper edge of cuff, with blue and No. 2 needles, cast on 35 (35, 37, 37, 39) stitches. Work even in knit 1, purl 1 ribbing for 4 rows. Change to No. 4 needles and work in stripe pattern until piece measures 1½ (1½, 2, 2, 2¼) inches, finishing with a purl row.

Next Row (Eyelet Row): Continuing in stripe pattern as established, knit 1; * yarn over, knit 2 together, knit 2; repeat from * across row. Purl even across next row. Then work two more complete stripes, finishing with a purl row, and cut yarn.

Divide for Foot: Next Row (right side): Slip first 11 (11, 11, 11, 12) stitches onto a stitch holder for one side of foot; attach yarn of appropriate color to continue in stripe pattern and knit next 13 (13, 15, 15, 15) stitches; slip remaining 11 (11, 11, 11, 12) stitches onto a stitch holder for other side of foot.

Shape Instep: Continuing in stripe pattern, work center 13 (13, 15, 15, 15) stitches until instep flap measures 2 (2, 2¼, 2½, 2¾) inches, finishing with a purl row. Cut yarn.

Shape Sides and Sole: Working from right side of piece, with blue and No. 2 needles, knit the 11 (11, 11, 11, 12) stitches from first stitch holder, pick up 14 (15, 16, 17, 18) stitches along side of instep flap, place a marker on needle, knit the 13 (13, 15, 15, 15) stitches along front edge of instep flap, place a marker on needle, pick up 14 (15, 16, 17, 18) stitches along other side of instep flap, knit the 11 (11, 11, 11, 12) stitches from second stitch holder—63 (65, 69, 71, 75) stitches. Then work even in garter stitch (knit each row) for 9 (9, 9, 11, 11) rows. (NOTE: Keep markers in place on needle while working these rows.)

Next Row (right side): Knit 2 together, knit to first marker, slip marker, knit 2 together, knit to 2 stitches before second marker, knit 2 together, slip marker, knit to last 2 stitches, knit last 2 stitches together—59 (61, 65, 67, 71) stitches. Work next row even in garter stitch. Repeat these 2 rows twice—51 (53, 57, 59, 63) stitches. Then work even in garter stitch for 2 (2, 4, 4, 4) rows. Bind off loosely.

Make second bootee in same manner.

FINISHING: Weave all remaining yarn ends into back of work. Sew center back and sole seams, working from wrong side of piece. Make drawstrings for the bootees by crocheting two 15-inch chains, using doubled strands of blue yarn. Lace a drawstring through the eyelets of each bootee.

Hooded Bunting and Mittens

SIZES: Directions are for size newborn-3 months. Changes for size 6–12 months are given in parentheses. Bunting measures approximately 24 (25¾) inches around chest.

MATERIALS: Sport yarn, 21 (27) ounces blue, 4 ounces white. Knitting needles No. 2 (or size needed to obtain gauge). Crochet hook size E. Large-eyed tapestry needle. One 16 (20) inch zipper.

GAUGE: 6 stitches = 1 inch; 12 rows = 1 inch (garter stitch).

NOTE: Bunting and mittens are worked throughout with two strands of yarn.

BUNTING

BACK: Beginning at lower edge, with two strands of blue, cast on 110 (122) stitches. Then work as follows:

STRIPE PATTERN: Row 1 (right side): With blue, knit even across row.
Rows 2–8: Knit even across each row.
Row 9: Knit 20 (24), knit 2 together, knit to last 22 (26) stitches, knit 2 together, knit remaining 20 (24) stitches—*108 (120) stitches.*
Rows 10–16: Knit even across each row. After completing Row 16, cut blue and attach white.
Row 17: With white, knit even across row.
Row 18: Purl even across row.
Row 19: Knit 20 (24), knit 2 together, knit to last 22

(26) stitches, knit 2 together, knit remaining 20 (24) stitches—*106 (118) stitches.*
Row 20: Purl even across row. Cut white and reattach blue. Repeat Rows 1–20 for stripe pattern, decreasing on Rows 9 and 19 as indicated until 74 (80) stitches remain. Then work even in stripe pattern as necessary, eliminating the decreases on Rows 9 and 19, until nine (twelve) white stripes have been completed. Cut white, reattach blue and work even in garter stitch (*knit each row*) until piece measures 18¼ (21½) inches, working last row on wrong side.
Shape Raglan Armholes: Continuing to work in garter stitch with blue, bind off 3 stitches at beginning of next 2 rows—*68 (74) stitches.* Then decrease 1 stitch at each side every other row 20 (22) times, working the decreases on the right side of the piece—*28 (30) stitches.* Bind off.

RIGHT FRONT: Beginning at lower edge, with two strands of blue, cast on 55 (61) stitches. Then work as follows:

STRIPE PATTERN: Row 1 (right side): With blue, knit even across row.
Rows 2–8: Knit even across each row.
Row 9: Knit to last 22 (26) stitches, knit 2 together, knit remaining 20 (24) stitches—*54 (60) stitches.*
Rows 10–16: Knit even across each row.
Row 17: Knit 3 (*front edge*), drop blue without cutting yarn and attach two strands of white; with white, knit remaining 51 (57) stitches.
Row 18: With white, purl to last 3 stitches; with blue, knit last 3 stitches (*front edge*).
Row 19: With blue, knit 3 (*front edge*); with white, knit to last 22 (26) stitches, knit 2 together, knit remaining 20 (24) stitches—*53 (59) stitches.*
Row 20: With white, purl to last 3 stitches; cut white; with blue, knit last 3 stitches (*front edge*). Repeat Rows 1–20 for stripe pattern, decreasing on Rows 9 and 19 as indicated until 37 (40) stitches remain. Then work even in stripe pattern as necessary, eliminating the decreases on Rows 9 and 19, until nine (twelve) white stripes have been completed. Cut white and work even in garter stitch with blue until piece measures same length as back to underarm, working last row on right side.
Shape Raglan Armhole: Continuing to work in garter stitch with blue, bind off 4 stitches at beginning of next row (*armhole edge*)—*33 (36) stitches.* Then decrease 1 stitch at armhole edge every other row 14 times, working the decreases on the right side of the piece—*19 (22) stitches.*
Shape Neck: Continuing in garter stitch, at neck edge bind off 6 (7) stitches once, 3 stitches once, 2 stitches

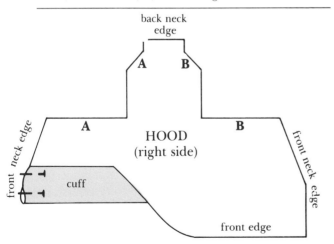

ASSEMBLING THE HOOD. Sew together corresponding edges (indicated by the same letter) for right back and left back seams. To form cuff, fold front edge as shown and pin to hold.

once and 1 stitch 2 times; at same time, continue to decrease 1 stitch at armhole edge every other row as before until only 2 stitches remain. Bind off.

LEFT FRONT: Beginning at lower edge, with two strands of blue, cast on 55 (61) stitches. Then work as follows:
STRIPE PATTERN: Row 1 (right side): With blue, knit even across row.
Rows 2–8: Knit even across each row.
Row 9: Knit 20 (24), knit 2 together, knit to end of row—*54 (60) stitches.*
Rows 10–16: Knit even across each row. After completing Row 16, drop blue without cutting yarn and attach two strands of white. (*NOTE: Carry original strands of blue along side edge of next 4 rows.*)
Row 17: With white, knit to last 3 stitches; drop white without cutting yarn and attach two new strands of blue; with blue, knit last 3 stitches (*front edge*).
Row 18: With blue, knit 3 (*front edge*), with white, purl to end of row.
Row 19: With white, knit 20 (24), knit 2 together, knit to last 3 stitches; with blue, knit last 3 stitches (*front edge—53 (59) stitches.*)
Row 20: With blue, knit 3 (*front edge*); with white, purl to end of row; cut white. Repeat Rows 1–20 for stripe pattern, decreasing on Rows 9 and 19 as indicated until 37 (40) stitches remain. (*NOTE: Work main portion of all remaining blue stripes with original strands of blue, and work the 3 stitches along front edge with the new strands of blue.*) Then work even in stripe pattern as necessary, eliminating the decreases on Rows 9 and 19, until nine (twelve) white stripes have been completed. Cut white as well as the blue strands used along front edge and work even in garter stitch with original strands of blue until piece measures same length as back to underarm, working last row on wrong side.
Shape Raglan Armhole: Continuing to work in garter stitch with blue, bind off 4 stitches at beginning of next row (*armhole edge*)—*33 (36) stitches.* Then decrease 1 stitch at armhole edge every other row 14 times, working the decreases on the right side of the piece—*19 (22) stitches.*
Shape Neck: Continuing in garter stitch, at neck edge bind off 6 (7) stitches once, 3 stitches once, 2 stitches once and 1 stitch 2 times; at same time, continue to decrease 1 stitch at armhole edge every other row as before until only 2 stitches remain. Bind off.

RIGHT SLEEVE: Beginning at lower edge, with two strands of blue, cast on 42 (44) stitches. Work even in garter stitch for 2 inches. Then, continuing in garter stitch, increase 1 stitch at each side every 10 rows 6 (8) times—*54 (60) stitches.* Work even until piece measures 7 (8) inches or desired length to underarm, working last row on wrong side.
Shape Raglan Cap: Bind off 4 stitches at beginning of next row (*front edge*) and 3 stitches at beginning of following row (*back edge*)—*47 (53) stitches.* Then decrease 1 stitch at each side every other row 18 (20) times, working the decreases on the right side of the piece—*11 (13) stitches.*
Next Row (wrong side): Knit even across row.
Next Row (right side): Bind off first 3 (4) stitches (*front edge*), knit to last 2 stitches, knit last 2 stitches together—*7 (8) stitches.*

Next Row: Knit even across row.
Next Row: Bind off first 3 (4) stitches (*front edge*), knit 1, knit last 2 stitches together—*3 stitches.*
Next Row: Knit even across row. Bind off.

LEFT SLEEVE: Work as for right sleeve to underarm.
Shape Raglan Cap: Bind off 3 stitches at beginning of next row (*back edge*) and 4 stitches at beginning of following row (*front edge*). Then decrease 1 stitch at each side every other row 18 (20) times, working the decreases on the right side of the piece—*11 (13) stitches.*
Next Row (wrong side): Bind off first 3 (4) stitches (*front edge*), knit remaining 7 (8) stitches—*8 (9) stitches.*
Next Row (right side): Knit first 2 stitches together, knit remaining 6 (7) stitches—*7 (8) stitches.*
Next Row: Bind off first 3 (4) stitches (*front edge*), knit remaining 3 stitches—*4 stitches.*
Next Row: Knit first 2 stitches together, knit remaining 2 stitches—*3 stitches.* Bind off.

HOOD: Beginning at front edge, with two strands of blue, cast on 100 (110) stitches. Work in garter stitch for 36 (40) rows. Then decrease 1 stitch at each side every 4 rows 12 (14) times—*76 (82) stitches.*
Shape Back: Bind off 27 (30) stitches at beginning of next 2 rows—*22 stitches.* Work even on remaining stitches for 2¼ (2¾) inches. Then bind off 1 stitch at each side every 6 rows 3 times—*16 stitches.* Work even on remaining stitches until back section of hood measures 4¼ (5) inches. Bind off.

FINISHING: Weave all remaining yarn ends into back of work. Block pieces lightly if necessary. Working from wrong side, sew sleeves to front and back sections. Then sew side and sleeve underarm seams. Stitch left back and right back seams of hood (*see diagram*); then fold front edge 2 inches to right side of hood to form a cuff and pin to hold. Working from wrong side, sew hood to neck edge of bunting. Sew zipper in place, using small, invisible stitches and allowing front edges of bunting to meet over zipper teeth. Finally, sew center front edges together below bottom stop of zipper and seam lower edge of bunting.

MITTENS

Beginning at cuff edge, with two strands of blue, cast on 38 (40) stitches. Work even in garter stitch (*knit each row*) for 1½ inches, working last row on wrong side.
Next Row (Eyelet Row): * Knit 2, yarn over, knit 2 together; repeat from * across row.
Next Row: Knit even across row—*38 (40) stitches.* Continue working in garter stitch until piece measures 3½ (4) inches, working last row on wrong side.
Next Row (right side): Continuing in garter stitch, decrease 4 stitches evenly across row—*34 (36) stitches.* Work next row even in garter stitch. Repeat these 2 rows 4 times—*18 (20) stitches.* Bind off.
  Make second mitten in same manner.

FINISHING: Weave all remaining yarn ends into back of work. Sewing from wrong side, stitch top and side seams of each mitten. Make drawstrings for the mittens by crocheting two 15-inch chains, using doubled strands of blue yarn. Lace a drawstring through the eyelets of each mitten.

Personalized Bib

SIZE: Bib measures approximately 8 inches by 9 inches.

MATERIALS: Baby or fingering yarn, 2 ounces pink, 2 ounces white. Knitting needles No. 4 (or size needed to obtain gauge). Crochet hook size C. Large-eyed tapestry needle.

GAUGE: 7 stitches = 1 inch; 9 rows = 1 inch (stockinette stitch).

FRONT: Beginning at lower edge, with pink, cast on 58 stitches. Work even in garter stitch (*knit each row*) for 8 rows. Then change to stockinette stitch (*knit 1 row, purl 1 row*), except continue to work first 6 stitches and last 6 stitches in garter stitch for side borders. Work even in this manner until piece measures 3 inches, working last row on wrong side.

Next Row (right side): With pink, knit first 6 stitches for side border; drop pink without cutting yarn and attach white; with white, knit next 46 stitches for main section of bib; drop white without cutting yarn and attach second strand of pink; with pink, knit last 6 stitches for side border. Continue working side borders in garter stitch with pink and remaining stitches in stockinette stitch with white until white stripe measures 3 inches, working last row on wrong side.

Next Row (right side): With first strand of pink, knit even across row, cutting white and second strand of pink. Then continue in pattern as established, working first 6 stitches and last 6 stitches in garter stitch for side border and remaining 46 stitches in stockinette stitch, until pink stripe measures 1 inch, working last row on wrong side.

Shape Neck: Next Row (right side): With pink, knit first 23 stitches; drop yarn without cutting it and attach another strand of pink; with new strand, bind off next 12 stitches, knit to end of row—*23 stitches each side.* Continuing in pattern and working both sides at same time with separate strands of pink, at each neck edge bind off 4 stitches once, 2 stitches once and 1 stitch 3 times—*14 stitches each side.* Now change to garter stitch and work even for 8 rows, working both sides at same time with separate strands of yarn. Bind off remaining stitches on each side.

Neckband: Working from right side of piece, with pink, pick up 44 stitches around neck edge. Work even in garter stitch for 2 rows. Bind off from wrong side of work.

FINISHING: Weave all remaining yarn ends into back of work. Block lightly if necessary. Using a doubled strand of pink yarn, crochet a chain of the length required to spell the baby's name. Place the chain on the white band of the bib, shaping it to form the letters of the name desired, and then pin to hold and sew it in place. Make ties for the bib by crocheting two 15-inch chains, using doubled strands of pink yarn. Sew one tie to each back neck corner of the bib.

Butterfly-Embroidered Dress, Pants and Bootees

Butterfly-Embroidered Dress, Pants and Bootees

SIZES: Directions are for size newborn–4 months. Changes for sizes 4–8, 8–12, 12–15 and 15–18 months are given in parentheses. Dress measures approximately 19 (20, 21, 21½, 22) inches around chest and 10½ (11¾, 12½, 13½, 14¾) inches from shoulder to bottom edge.

MATERIALS: Baby or fingering yarn, 7 (7, 7, 9, 9) ounces white, 4 ounces red, scraps of midnight blue and yellow. Knitting needles Nos. 1 and 2 (or size needed to obtain gauge). Crochet hook size B. Two stitch holders. Large-eyed tapestry needle. Three small buttons. Two-thirds yard ½-inch-wide elastic.

GAUGE: 8 stitches = 1 inch; 11 rows = 1 inch (stockinette stitch, No. 2 needles).

SEED STITCH PATTERN: Work on a multiple of 2 stitches as follows:
Row 1: * Knit 1, purl 1; repeat from * across row.
Row 2: * Purl 1, knit 1; repeat from * across row. Repeat these 2 rows for pattern.

DRESS

BACK: Lower Border: With red and No. 1 needles, loosely cast on 120 (128, 132, 140, 144) stitches. Work even in seed stitch pattern for 10 rows. Cut red.
Body: Change to No. 2 needles, attach white and work in stockinette stitch (*knit 1 row, purl 1 row*) as follows:
Row 1 (right side): Knit even across row.
Row 2 (wrong side): Purl 26, place a marker on needle, purl to last 26 stitches, place a marker on needle, purl remaining 26 stitches.
Row 3: Knit first 2 stitches together, knit to first marker, slip marker, slip next stitch, knit 1, pass slipped stitch over knitted stitch, knit to 2 stitches before second marker, knit 2 together, slip marker, knit to last 2 stitches, knit last 2 stitches together—*116 (124, 128, 136, 140) stitches.*
Row 4: Purl even across row, slipping markers.
Row 5: Knit even across row, slipping markers.
Row 6: Purl even across row, slipping markers.
Row 7: Knit to first marker, slip marker, slip next stitch, knit 1, pass slipped stitch over knitted stitch, knit to last 2 stitches before second marker, knit 2 together, slip marker, knit remaining stitches—*114 (122, 126, 134, 138) stitches.* Repeat Rows 3–7, 6 (7, 7, 8, 8) times, removing markers after completing last decrease row—*78 (80, 84, 86, 90) stitches.* Then work even in stockinette stitch until piece measures 6½ (7½, 8, 9, 9¾) inches or desired length to underarm, finishing with a purl row.
Shape Raglan Armholes: Continuing in stockinette stitch, bind off 3 stitches at beginning of next 2 rows—*72 (74, 78, 80, 84) stitches.* Then decrease 1 stitch at each side every other row 5 times, working the decreases on the knit rows—*62 (64, 68, 70, 74) stitches.*
Divide for Center Back Opening: Next Row (wrong side): Purl first 29 (30, 32, 33, 35) stitches, knit 2; drop yarn without cutting it and attach another strand of white; with new strand, knit 2, purl remaining 29 (30, 32, 33, 35) stitches—*31 (32, 34, 35, 37) stitches each side.* Working both sides at same time with separate strands of yarn, continue in stockinette stitch, except work the 2 stitches on each side of center back opening in garter stitch (*knit on all rows*); and at same time continue to decrease 1 stitch at each armhole edge every other row 17 (18, 20, 21, 23) times—*14 stitches each side.* Bind off remaining stitches on each side.

FRONT: Work as for back to underarm.
Shape Raglan Armholes: Continuing in stockinette stitch, bind off 3 stitches at beginning of next 2 rows—*72 (74, 78, 80, 84) stitches.* Then decrease 1 stitch at each side every other row 12 (13, 14, 15, 17) times, working the decreases on the knit rows—*48 (48, 50, 50, 50) stitches.* Purl next row.
Shape Neck: Next Row (right side): Knit first 2 stitches together, knit next 17 (17, 18, 18, 18) stitches; drop yarn without cutting it and attach another strand of white; with new strand, bind off next 10 stitches, knit to last 2 stitches, knit last 2 stitches together—*18 (18, 19, 19, 19) stitches each side.* Working both sides at same time with separate strands of yarn, at each neck edge bind off 3 stitches once, 2 stitches once and 1 stitch 4 times; at same time, continue to decrease 1 stitch at each armhole edge every other row as before until only 2 stitches remain on each side. Bind off remaining stitches on each side.

RIGHT SLEEVE: Beginning at lower edge, with red and No. 1 needles, cast on 46 (48, 52, 54, 58) stitches. Work even in seed stitch pattern for 6 rows. Cut red. Change to No. 2 needles, attach white and work in stockinette stitch, increasing 1 stitch at each side every other row 6 times—*58 (60, 64, 66, 70) stitches.* Then work even in stockinette stitch until piece measures 2 inches, finishing with a purl row.
Shape Raglan Cap: Continuing in stockinette stitch, bind off 3 stitches at beginning of next 2 rows—*52 (54, 58, 60, 64) stitches.* Then decrease 1 stitch at each side every other row 20 (21, 23, 24, 26) times, working the decreases on the knit rows—*12 stitches.* Purl next row.
Next Row (right side): Bind off first 3 stitches (*front edge*), knit 6, knit last 2 stitches together—*8 stitches.*
Next Row (wrong side): Purl even across row.

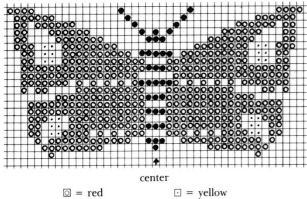

center

☑ = red   ⊡ = yellow
◙ = midnight blue   ☐ = background

BUTTERFLY DESIGN CHART.

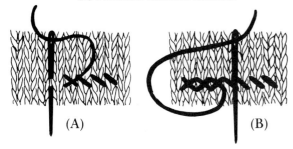

(A)   (B)

CROSS STITCH EMBROIDERY. Thread a blunt-tipped tapestry needle with a single strand of yarn of desired color. Working from right to left across a single row of knitted stitches, make a diagonal stitch over each knitted stitch to be embroidered in that color (*fig. A*). At end of row, reverse directions and work back over the original series of stitches (*fig. B*). Repeat as necessary, following the design chart for placement of stitches and colors.

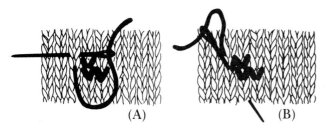

(A)   (B)

DUPLICATE STITCH EMBROIDERY. Thread a blunt-tipped tapestry needle with a single strand of yarn of desired color. Bring needle and yarn up from wrong side of work through center of the base of knitted stitch to be embroidered. Then insert needle from right to left under both strands of knitted stitch directly above and pull yarn through (*fig. A*). Reinsert needle into base of stitch just to left of point where yarn was originally brought up, and pull yarn through to wrong side (*fig. B*). Repeat as necessary, following the design chart for placement of stitches and colors.

Next Row: Bind off first 3 stitches (*front edge*), knit 2, knit last 2 stitches together—*4 stitches.*
Next Row: Purl even across row. Bind off.

LEFT SLEEVE: Work as for right sleeve to underarm.
Shape Raglan Cap: Continuing in stockinette stitch, bind off 3 stitches at beginning of next 2 rows—*52 (54, 58, 60, 64) stitches.* Then decrease 1 stitch at each side every other row 20 (21, 23, 24, 26) times, working the decreases on the knit rows—*12 stitches.*

Next Row (wrong side): Bind off first 3 stitches (*front edge*), purl remaining 8 stitches—*9 stitches.*
Next Row (right side): Knit first 2 stitches together, knit remaining 8 stitches—*8 stitches.*
Next Row: Bind off first 3 stitches (*front edge*), purl remaining 4 stitches—*5 stitches.*
Next Row: Knit first 2 stitches together, knit remaining 3 stitches—*4 stitches.* Bind off.

FINISHING: Weave all remaining yarn ends into back of work. Block pieces lightly if necessary.

BUTTERFLY EMBROIDERY: With blunt-tipped tapestry needle and single strands of red, yellow and blue yarn, work butterfly design in cross stitch or duplicate stitch embroidery (*see diagrams*) across chest of dress front, following the charted design for placement of colors.
Working from wrong side, sew sleeves to front and back sections. Then sew side and sleeve underarm seams.

NECKBAND: Working from right side of garment, with red and No. 1 needles, pick up 77 (81, 83, 85, 87) stitches around neck edge. Work even in knit 1, purl 1 ribbing for 8 rows. Bind off in ribbing from wrong side of work. Sew three yarn loops evenly spaced along one edge of center back opening. Sew buttons in position along opposite edge of opening.

PANTS

FRONT: Beginning at lower edge of crotch, with white and No. 2 needles, cast on 16 (18, 20, 22, 24) stitches. Work even in stockinette stitch (*knit 1 row, purl 1 row*) for 24 (26, 28, 28, 30) rows. Increase 1 stitch at each side of next 6 rows—*28 (30, 32, 34, 36) stitches.* Then cast on 28 (28, 29, 29, 30) stitches at end of next 2 rows—*84 (86, 90, 92, 96) stitches.* Continue working in stockinette stitch, decreasing 1 stitch at each side every 3 rows 4 times—*76 (78, 82, 84, 88) stitches.* Then work even until side edges measure 4¾ (5, 5½, 5¾, 6½) inches, finishing with a purl row. Cut white.
Waistband: Next Row (right side): Change to No. 1 needles, attach red and work in knit 1, purl 1 ribbing for ¾ inch. Bind off loosely in ribbing.

BACK: Beginning at lower edge of crotch, with white and No. 2 needles, cast on 16 (18, 20, 22, 24) stitches. Work in stockinette stitch, increasing 1 stitch at each side of first 34 (34, 35, 35, 36) rows—*84 (86, 90, 92, 96) stitches.* Then decrease 1 stitch at each side every 3 rows 4 times—*76 (78, 82, 84, 88) stitches.* Work even until side edges of piece measure 4¾ (5, 5½, 5¾, 6½) inches, finishing with a purl row.
Shape Back (Short Rows): Row 1: Knit first 68 (70, 74, 76, 80) stitches, turn (*do not work last 8 stitches of row*).
Row 2: Slip first stitch, purl next 59 (61, 65, 67, 71) stitches, turn (*do not work last 8 stitches of row*).
Row 3: Slip first stitch, knit next 51 (53, 57, 59, 63) stitches, turn (*do not work last 16 stitches of row*).
Row 4: Slip first stitch, purl next 43 (45, 49, 51, 55) stitches, turn (*do not work last 16 stitches of row*).
Row 5: Slip first stitch, knit next 35 (37, 41, 43, 47) stitches, turn (*do not work last 24 stitches of row*).
Row 6: Slip first stitch, purl next 27 (29, 33, 35, 39) stitches, turn (*do not work last 24 stitches of row*).

Row 7: Slip first stitch, knit next 19 (21, 25, 27, 31) stitches, turn (do not work last 32 stitches of row).
Row 8: Slip first stitch, purl next 11 (13, 17, 19, 23) stitches, turn (do not work last 32 stitches of row).
Row 9: Slip first stitch, knit across to end of row, working each slipped stitch together with stitch directly below it.
Row 10: Purl across entire row, working each remaining slipped stitch together with stitch directly below it—76 (78, 82, 84, 88) stitches. Cut white.
Waistband: Next Row (right side): Change to No. 1 needles, attach red and work in knit 1, purl 1 ribbing for ¾ inch. Bind off loosely in ribbing.

FINISHING: Weave all remaining yarn ends into back of work. Block pieces lightly if necessary. Working from wrong side, seam front and back sections together at crotch.

LEG RIBBING: Working from right side of garment, with red and No. 1 needles, pick up 73 (77, 81, 85, 89) stitches around edge of one leg. Work even in knit 1, purl 1 ribbing for 1½ inches. Bind off loosely in ribbing. Repeat around edge of other leg.

Sew side seams, working from wrong side of garment. Fold each leg ribbing in half to wrong side and loosely stitch bound-off edge in place. Then cut elastic to fit, stitch the ends together, and sew to inside of waistband.

BOOTEES

Beginning at upper edge of cuff, with red and No. 1 needles, loosely cast on 38 (40, 42, 44, 46) stitches. Work even in knit 1, purl 1 ribbing for 6 rows. Cut red. Change to No. 2 needles, attach white and work in stockinette stitch (knit 1 row, purl 1 row) for 20 rows.
Divide for Foot: Next Row (right side): Bind off first 12 (12, 13, 13, 14) stitches for one side of foot, knit remaining 25 (27, 28, 30, 31) stitches—26 (28, 29, 31, 32) stitches.
Next Row (wrong side): Bind off first 12 (12, 13, 13, 14) stitches for other side of foot, purl remaining 13 (15, 15, 17, 17) stitches—14 (16, 16, 18, 18) stitches.
Shape Instep: Continuing in stockinette stitch, work the 14 (16, 16, 18, 18) stitches remaining on needle until instep flap measures 2 (2, 2¼, 2½, 2¾) inches. Bind off.
Shape Sides and Sole: Working from right side of piece, with red and No. 1 needles, pick up 11 (11, 12, 12, 13) stitches along bound-off edge of first side of foot, pick up 16 (17, 18, 20, 21) stitches along side of instep flap, place a marker on needle, pick up 12 (14, 14, 16, 16) stitches along front edge of instep flap, place a marker on needle, pick up 16 (17, 18, 20, 21) stitches along other side of instep flap, and then pick up 11 (11, 12, 12, 13) stitches along bound-off edge of other side of foot—66 (70, 74, 80, 84) stitches. Work even in garter stitch (knit each row) for 7 (7, 9, 9, 11) rows. (NOTE: Keep markers in place on needle while working these rows.)
Next Row (right side): Knit 2 together, knit to first marker, slip marker, knit 2 together, knit to 2 stitches before second marker, knit 2 together, slip marker, knit to last 2 stitches, knit last 2 stitches together—62 (66, 70, 76, 80) stitches. Work next row even in garter stitch. Repeat these 2 rows 3 (3, 4, 4, 4) times—50 (54, 54, 60, 64) stitches. Then work 2 rows even in garter stitch. Bind off loosely.

Make second bootee in same manner.

FINISHING: Weave all remaining yarn ends into back of work. Sew center back and sole seams, working from wrong side of piece. Make drawstrings for the bootees by crocheting two 15-inch chains, using doubled strands of red yarn. Using a blunt-tipped tapestry needle, weave a drawstring in and out of each bootee around the ankle.

Striped Cap, Scarf and Mittens

SIZES: Directions are for size 3 months. Changes for sizes 6, 9, 12 and 15 months are given in parentheses.

MATERIALS: Baby or fingering yarn, 2 (2, 2, 4, 4) ounces light blue, 2 ounces white, 2 ounces medium blue. Knitting needles No. 3 (or size needed to obtain gauge). Crochet hook size B. Large-eyed tapestry needle.

GAUGE: 15 stitches = 2 inches (garter stitch).

CAP

With light blue, cast on 108 (112, 114, 116, 118) stitches. Work even in knit 1, purl 1 ribbing for 4 rows. Then change to garter stitch (*knit each row*) and work in stripe pattern as follows, cutting and joining colors as needed: 2 rows white, 6 rows medium blue, 2 rows white and 6 rows light blue. Repeat stripe pattern as necessary until piece measures 4 (4¼, 4½, 4¾, 5) inches, working last row on wrong side. Then, continuing in garter stitch and stripe pattern for remainder of piece, work as follows:

Shape Crown: Row 1 (right side): Knit, decreasing 8 (2, 4, 6, 8) stitches evenly across row—*100 (110, 110, 110, 110) stitches.*
Row 2 (wrong side): Knit even across row.
Row 3: * Knit 2 together, knit 8; repeat from * across row—*90 (99, 99, 99, 99) stitches.*
Row 4: Knit even across row.
Row 5: * Knit 2 together, knit 7; repeat from * across row—*80 (88, 88, 88, 88) stitches.*
Row 6: Knit even across row.
Row 7: * Knit 2 together, knit 6; repeat from * across row—*70 (77, 77, 77, 77) stitches.*
Row 8: Knit even across row.
Row 9: * Knit 2 together, knit 5; repeat from * across row—*60 (66, 66, 66, 66) stitches.*
Row 10: Knit even across row.
Row 11: * Knit 2 together, knit 4; repeat from * across row—*50 (55, 55, 55, 55) stitches.*
Row 12: Knit even across row.
Row 13: * Knit 2 together, knit 3; repeat from * across row—*40 (44, 44, 44, 44) stitches.*
Row 14: Knit even across row.
Row 15: * Knit 2 together, knit 2; repeat from * across row—*30 (33, 33, 33, 33) stitches.*
Row 16: Knit even across row.
Row 17: * Knit 2 together, knit 1; repeat from * across row—*20 (22, 22, 22, 22) stitches.*
Row 18: Knit even across row.
Row 19: * Knit 2 together; repeat from * across row—*10 (11, 11, 11, 11) stitches.* Cut yarn, leaving a 12-inch end.

Thread yarn end onto a blunt-tipped tapestry needle and draw through all stitches on knitting needle. Pull tight and fasten securely on wrong side of work. Working from wrong side of piece, sew side edges together for center back seam.
Ear Flaps: Working with cap right side out and seam at center back, with light blue, pick up 25 (25, 27, 27, 29) stitches along edge at one side of cap. Then work as follows:
Row 1 (wrong side): Purl 1; * knit 1, purl 1; repeat from * across row.
Row 2: Knit 1, purl 1, slip next stitch as if to purl, purl 1, pass slipped stitch over purled stitch, knit 1; * purl 1, knit 1; repeat from * to last 4 stitches; knit 2 together, purl 1, knit 1—*23 (23, 25, 25, 27) stitches.*
Row 3: Purl 1, knit 1, purl 2, knit 1; * purl 1, knit 1; repeat from * to last 4 stitches; purl 2, knit 1, purl 1.
Row 4: Knit 1, purl 1, slip next stitch, knit 1, pass slipped stitch over knitted stitch, purl 1; * knit 1, purl 1; repeat from * to last 4 stitches; knit 2 together, purl 1, knit 1—*21 (21, 23, 23, 25) stitches.*
Row 5: Purl 1; * knit 1, purl 1; repeat from * across row. Repeat Rows 2–5 until only 7 stitches remain, finishing on right side of piece with either Row 2 or Row 4.
Next Row (wrong side): Purl 1; * knit 1, purl 1; repeat from * across row.
Next Row (right side): Knit 1, purl 1, slip next stitch, knit 2 together, pass slipped stitch over knitted stitch, purl 1, knit 1—*5 stitches.*
Next Row: Purl 1, knit 1, purl 1, knit 1, purl 1.
Next Row: Knit 1, slip next stitch as if to purl, purl 2 together, pass slipped stitch over purled stitch, knit 1—*3 stitches.*
Next Row: Purl 1, knit 1, purl 1.
Next Row: Slip first stitch, knit last 2 stitches together, pass slipped stitch over knitted stitch; end off.

Make second ear flap in same manner, working on opposite side of cap.

FINISHING: Weave all remaining yarn ends into back of work. Make ties for the cap by crocheting two 15-inch chains, using doubled strands of light blue yarn. Sew one tie to the end of each ear flap. Make a pompon with light blue yarn and sew to top of cap.

SCARF

With light blue, cast on 3 stitches. Then work in garter stitch (*knit each row*) as follows:
Row 1 (right side): Knit 1, knit in front and in back of next stitch, knit 1—*4 stitches.*
Row 2 (wrong side): Knit even across row.

Row 3: Knit 2; pick up a loop between stitches, twist and then knit into loop; knit 2—*5 stitches.*
Row 4: Knit even across row.
Row 5: Knit 1, knit in front and in back of next stitch, knit to last 2 stitches, knit in front and in back of next stitch, knit 1—*7 stitches.*
Row 6: Knit even across row. Repeat Rows 5–6, 8 (8, 9, 10, 11) times—*23 (23, 25, 27, 29) stitches.* Then work next 6 (6, 6, 10, 10) rows even in garter stitch.

STRIPE PATTERN: Continuing in garter stitch, work stripe pattern as follows, cutting and joining colors as needed: 4 rows white, 10 rows medium blue, 4 rows white and 26 (30, 32, 34, 36) rows light blue. Repeat stripe pattern 6 times. Then work stripes of 4 rows white, 10 rows medium blue, 4 rows white and 6 (6, 6, 10, 10) rows light blue.
Next Row (right side): Continuing in garter stitch with light blue, knit 1, knit 2 together, knit to last 3 stitches, knit 2 together, knit 1—*21 (21, 23, 25, 27) stitches.* Knit even across next row. Repeat these 2 rows 8 (8, 9, 10, 11) times—*5 stitches.*
Next Row (right side): Knit 1, knit 2 together, knit 2—*4 stitches.*
Next Row: Knit even across row.
Next Row: Knit 1, knit 2 together, knit 1—*3 stitches.* Bind off.

FINISHING: Weave all remaining yarn ends into back of work. Block scarf lightly if necessary.

MITTENS

Beginning at cuff edge, with light blue, cast on 42 (42, 44, 44, 46) stitches. Work in garter stitch (*knit each row*) and stripe pattern as follows, cutting and joining colors as needed: 6 rows light blue, 2 rows white, 6 rows medium blue and 2 rows white. Repeat stripe pattern as necessary until piece measures 1½ inches, working last row on wrong side.
Next Row (Eyelet Row): Continuing in stripe pattern as established, * knit 1, yarn over, knit 2 together; repeat from * across row.
Next Row: Knit even across row—*42 (42, 44, 44, 46) stitches.* Then continue working even in garter stitch and stripe pattern until piece measures 3½ (3½, 3¾, 4, 4) inches, working last row on wrong side.
Next Row (right side): Continuing in garter stitch and stripe pattern, decrease 4 stitches evenly across row—*38 (38, 40, 40, 42) stitches.* Work next row even in garter stitch. Repeat these 2 rows 4 times—*22 (22, 24, 24, 26) stitches.* Bind off.
Make second mitten in same manner.

FINISHING: Weave all remaining yarn ends into back of work. Sewing from wrong side, stitch top and side seams of each mitten. Make drawstrings for the mittens by crocheting two 15-inch chains, using doubled strands of light blue yarn. Lace a drawstring through the eyelets of each mitten.

Eyelet Rib Cardigan, Romper, Cap and Bootees

SIZES: Directions are for size newborn–4 months. Changes for sizes 4–8 and 8–12 months are given in parentheses. Cardigan measures approximately 18¾ (20, 21) inches around chest.

MATERIALS: Baby or fingering yarn, 9 (11, 13) ounces pink. Knitting needles Nos. 1 and 2 (or size needed to obtain gauge). Crochet hook size B. Two stitch holders. Large-eyed tapestry needle. Ten buttons.

GAUGE: 8 stitches = 1 inch; 11 rows = 1 inch (pattern stitch, No. 2 needles)

EYELET RIB PATTERN: Work on a multiple of 4 stitches plus 1 as follows:
Row 1 (right side): * Knit 1, purl 3; repeat from * to last stitch; knit 1.
Row 2 (wrong side): * Purl 1, knit 3; repeat from * to last stitch; purl 1.
Row 3: * Knit 1, purl 2 together, yarn over, purl 1; repeat from * to last stitch; knit 1.
Row 4: * Purl 1, knit 3; repeat from * to last stitch; purl 1.
Row 5: * Knit 1, purl 3; repeat from * to last stitch; knit 1.
Row 6: * Purl 1, knit 3; repeat from * to last stitch; purl 1. Repeat Rows 1–6 for pattern.

CARDIGAN

BACK: Beginning at lower edge, with No. 1 needles, cast on 77 (81, 85) stitches. Work even in garter stitch (*knit each row*) for 9 rows. Then change to No. 2 needles and work in eyelet rib pattern until piece measures 5¾ (6½, 7½) inches or desired length to underarm, working last row on wrong side.
Shape Raglan Armholes: Continuing in eyelet rib pattern as established, bind off 3 stitches at beginning of next 2 rows—*71 (75, 79) stitches*. Then decrease 1 stitch at each side every other row 21 (23, 25) times, working the decreases on the right side of the piece—*29 stitches*. Bind off.

RIGHT FRONT: Beginning at lower edge, with No. 1 needles, cast on 37 (41, 45) stitches. Work even in garter stitch for 9 rows. Then change to No. 2 needles and work in eyelet rib pattern until piece measures same length as back to underarm, working last row on right side.
Shape Raglan Armhole: Continuing in eyelet rib pattern as established, bind off 3 stitches at beginning of next row (*armhole edge*)—*34 (38, 42) stitches*. Then decrease 1 stitch at armhole edge every other row 11 (13, 15) times, working the decreases on the right side of the piece—*23 (25, 27) stitches*.
Shape Neck: Continuing in pattern as established, at neck edge bind off 5 (6, 6) stitches once, 3 stitches once, 2 stitches once and 1 stitch 3 (3, 4) times; at same time, continue to decrease 1 stitch at armhole edge every other row as before until only 2 stitches remain. Bind off.

LEFT FRONT: Beginning at lower edge, with No. 1 needles, cast on 37 (41, 45) stitches. Work even in garter stitch for 9 rows. Then change to No. 2 needles and work in eyelet rib pattern until piece measures same length as back to underarm, working last row on wrong side.
Shape Raglan Armhole: Continuing in eyelet rib pattern as established, bind off 3 stitches at beginning of next row (*armhole edge*)—*34 (38, 42) stitches*. Then decrease 1 stitch at armhole edge every other row 11 (13, 15) times, working the decreases on the right side of the piece—*23 (25, 27) stitches*.
Shape Neck: Continuing in pattern as established, at neck edge bind off 5 (6, 6) stitches once, 3 stitches once, 2 stitches once and 1 stitch 3 (3, 4) times; at same time, continue to decrease 1 stitch at armhole edge every other row as before until only 2 stitches remain. Bind off.

RIGHT SLEEVE: Beginning at lower edge, with No. 1 needles, cast on 41 (45, 49) stitches. Work even in garter stitch for 9 rows. Then change to No. 2 needles and work in eyelet rib pattern, increasing 1 stitch at each side every 6 rows 8 times—*57 (61, 65) stitches*. Then work even in pattern until piece measures 5¾ (6½, 7½) inches or desired length to underarm, working last row on wrong side in same pattern row as on back section at underarm.
Shape Raglan Cap: Continuing in eyelet rib pattern as established, bind off 3 stitches at beginning of next 2 rows—*51 (55, 59) stitches*. Then decrease 1 stitch at each side every other row 19 (21, 23) times, working the decreases on the right side of the piece—*13 stitches*.
Next Row (wrong side): Work even in pattern across row.
Next Row (right side): Bind off first 3 stitches (*front edge*), work in pattern to last 2 stitches, work last 2 stitches together—*9 stitches*.
Next Row: Work even in pattern across row.
Next Row: Bind off first 4 stitches (*front edge*), work in pattern to last 2 stitches, work last 2 stitches together—*4 stitches*.
Next Row: Work even in pattern across row. Bind off.

Eyelet Rib Cardigan, Romper, Cap and Bootees

LEFT SLEEVE: Work as for right sleeve to underarm.
Shape Raglan Cap: Continuing in eyelet rib pattern as established, bind off 3 stitches at beginning of next 2 rows—*51 (55, 59) stitches.* Then decrease 1 stitch at each side every other row 19 (21, 23) times, working the decreases on the right side of the piece—*13 stitches.*
Next Row (wrong side): Bind off first 3 stitches (*front edge*), work remaining 9 stitches in pattern—*10 stitches.*
Next Row (right side): Work first 2 stitches together, work remaining 8 stitches in pattern—*9 stitches.*
Next Row: Bind off first 4 stitches (*front edge*), work remaining 4 stitches in pattern—*5 stitches.*
Next Row: Work first 2 stitches together, work remaining 3 stitches in pattern—*4 stitches.* Bind off.

FINISHING: Weave all remaining yarn ends into back of work. Block pieces lightly if necessary. Working from wrong side, sew sleeves to front and back sections. Then sew side and sleeve underarm seams.

NECKBAND: Working from right side of garment, with No. 1 needles, pick up 80 (84, 88) stitches around neck edge. Work even in garter stitch for 9 rows. Bind off.

LEFT FRONT BAND: Working from right side of garment, with No. 1 needles, pick up stitches evenly along left front edge. Work even in garter stitch for 9 rows. Bind off.

RIGHT FRONT BAND: Work as for left front band until 4 rows of garter stitch have been completed. With pins, mark position of six buttonholes evenly spaced along front edge, inserting top pin ½ inch from neck edge and bottom pin ½ inch from lower edge.
Next Row (Buttonhole Row): * Knit to 1 stitch before pin marker, bind off next 2 stitches; repeat from * 5 times; knit to end of row.
Next Row: * Knit to bound-off stitches, cast on 2 stitches directly over bound-off stitches; repeat from * 5 times; knit to end of row. Then work 3 rows even in garter stitch. Bind off.
    Sew buttons in position on left front band.
    (*NOTE: For a boy's sweater, make buttonholes on left front band instead of on right front band.*)

ROMPER

BACK: Beginning at lower edge of crotch, with No. 2 needles, cast on 21 (23, 25) stitches. Work in stockinette stitch (*knit 1 row, purl 1 row*), increasing 1 stitch at each side of first 31 (32, 33) rows—*83 (87, 91) stitches.* Then decrease 1 stitch at each side every inch 3 times—*77 (81, 85) stitches.* Work even until side edges of piece measure 6¼ (6½, 7) inches, finishing with a purl row.
Shape Back (Short Rows) Row 1: Knit first 71 (75, 79) stitches, turn (*do not work last 6 stitches of row*).
Row 2: Slip first stitch, purl next 64 (68, 72) stitches, turn (*do not work last 6 stitches of row*).
Row 3: Slip first stitch, knit next 58 (62, 66) stitches, turn (*do not work last 12 stitches of row*).
Row 4: Slip first stitch, purl next 52 (56, 60) stitches, turn (*do not work last 12 stitches of row*).
Row 5: Slip first stitch, knit next 46 (50, 54) stitches, turn (*do not work last 18 stitches of row*).
Row 6: Slip first stitch, purl next 40 (44, 48) stitches, turn (*do not work last 18 stitches of row*).
Row 7: Slip first stitch, knit next 34 (38, 42) stitches, turn (*do not work last 24 stitches of row*).

Row 8: Slip first stitch, purl next 28 (32, 36) stitches, turn (*do not work last 24 stitches of row*).
Row 9: Slip first stitch, knit across to end of row, working each slipped stitch together with stitch directly below it.
Row 10: Purl across entire row, working each remaining slipped stitch together with stitch directly below it—*77 (81, 85) stitches.* Then change to eyelet rib pattern and work even until side edges of piece measure 7 (7½, 8¼) inches or desired length to underarm, working last row on wrong side.
Shape Armholes: Continuing in eyelet rib pattern as established, bind off 6 (7, 7) stitches at beginning of next 2 rows, 3 stitches at beginning of next 2 rows, 2 stitches at beginning of next 2 rows and 1 stitch at beginning of next 8 (8, 10) rows—*47 (49, 51) stitches.*
Shape Neck: Next Row (right side): Continuing in eyelet rib pattern as established, work first 16 (17, 18) stitches; drop yarn without cutting it and attach another strand of pink; with new strand, bind off next 15 stitches, work to end of row—*16 (17, 18) stitches each side.* Working both sides at same time with separate strands of yarn, at each neck edge bind off 3 stitches once, 2 stitches once and 1 stitch 5 times—*6 (7, 8) stitches each side.* Then work even on both sides until armholes measure 4 (4¼, 4¾) inches. Bind off remaining stitches on each side.

FRONT: Beginning at lower edge of crotch, with No. 2 needles, cast on 21 (23, 25) stitches. Work even in stockinette stitch for 2 (2, 2¼) inches, finishing with a purl row. Increase 1 stitch at each side of next 6 rows—*33 (35, 37) stitches.* Then cast on 25 (26, 27) stitches at end of next 2 rows—*83 (87, 91) stitches.* Continue working in stockinette stitch, decreasing 1 stitch at each side every inch 3 times—*77 (81, 85) stitches.* Then work even until side edges measure same length as side edges of back to first eyelet rib pattern row, finishing with a purl row. Now change to eyelet rib pattern and work even until side edges measure same as side edges of back to underarm, working last row on wrong side in same pattern row as on back.
Shape Armholes: Continuing in eyelet rib pattern as established, bind off 6 (7, 7) stitches at beginning of next 2 rows, 3 stitches at beginning of next 2 rows, 2 stitches at beginning of next 2 rows and 1 stitch at beginning of next 8 (8, 10) rows—*47 (49, 51) stitches.*
Shape Neck: Next Row (right side): Continuing in eyelet rib pattern as established, work first 16 (17, 18) stitches; drop yarn without cutting it and attach another strand of pink; with new strand, bind off next 15 stitches, work to end of row—*16 (17, 18) stitches each side.* Working both sides at same time with separate strands of yarn, at each neck edge bind off 3 stitches once, 2 stitches once and 1 stitch 5 times—*6 (7, 8) stitches each side.* Then work even on both sides until armholes measure 4¼ (4½, 5) inches. Bind off remaining stitches on each side.

FINISHING: Weave all remaining yarn ends into back of work. Block pieces lightly if necessary. Sew side seams, working from wrong side of garment.

LEG RIBBING: Working from right side of garment, with No. 1 needles, pick up 76 (80, 84) stitches around edge of one leg. Work even in knit 1, purl 1 ribbing for 1½ inches. Bind off loosely in ribbing. Repeat around edge of other leg. Sew crotch seam, working from wrong side of garment. Then fold each leg ribbing in half to wrong side and loosely stitch bound-off edge in place.

ARMHOLE RIBBING: Working from right side of garment, with No. 1 needles, pick up 102 (106, 110) stitches around edge of one armhole. Work even in knit 1, purl 1 ribbing for ½ inch. Bind off in ribbing from wrong side of work. Repeat around edge of other armhole.

NECKLINE RIBBING: Working from right side of garment, with No. 1 needles, pick up 102 (110, 118) stitches around front neck edge. Work even in knit 1, purl 1 ribbing for ½ inch. Bind off in ribbing from wrong side of work. Repeat around back neck edge.

ARMHOLE AND NECKLINE EDGING: Beginning and ending at side seam intersection of one armhole, with size B crochet hook, work 1 round of single crochet stitches around entire upper edge of garment, making two chain-stitch buttonhole loops along top edge of each front shoulder strap. Sew buttons in position on back shoulder straps.

CAP

Beginning at top of crown, with No. 2 needles, cast on 6 stitches.
Row 1 (right side): Knit even across row.
Row 2: Knit 1; * knit in front and in back of next stitch (*increase 1 stitch*); repeat from * to last 2 stitches; knit 2—*9 stitches*.
Row 3: Knit even across row.
Row 4: Knit 1; * knit in front and in back of next stitch; repeat from * to last stitch; knit 1—*16 stitches*.
Row 5: Knit even across row.
Row 6: * Knit 1, knit in front and in back of next stitch; repeat from * to last 2 stitches; knit 2—*23 stitches*.
Row 7: Knit even across row.
Row 8: Knit 1; * knit in front and in back of next stitch, knit 2; repeat from * to last 3 stitches; knit 3—*30 stitches*.
Row 9: Knit even across row.
Row 10: Knit 1; * knit in front and in back of next stitch, knit 3; repeat from * to last 4 stitches; knit 4—*37 stitches*.
Row 11: Knit even across row.
Row 12: Knit 1, * knit in front and in back of next stitch, knit 4; repeat from * to last 5 stitches; knit 5—*44 stitches*.
Row 13: Knit even across row.
Row 14: Knit 1; * knit in front and in back of next stitch, knit 5; repeat from * to last 6 stitches; knit 6—*51 stitches*.
Row 15: Knit even across row.
Row 16: Knit 1; * knit in front and in back of next stitch, knit 6; repeat from * to last 7 stitches; knit 7—*58 stitches*.
Row 17: Knit even across row.
Row 18: Knit 1; * knit in front and in back of next stitch; repeat from * to last stitch; knit 1—*114 stitches*.
Row 19: Knit even across row.
Row 20: Knit, increasing 3 (3, 7) stitches evenly across row—*117 (117, 121) stitches*. Then change to eyelet rib pattern and work even for 4 (4¼, 4½) inches.
Next Row: Continuing in eyelet rib pattern as established, bind off first 4 stitches (*back edge*), work next 31 stitches in pattern, bind off next 47 (47, 51) stitches (*front edge*), work next 31 stitches in pattern, bind off last 4 stitches (*back edge*); cut yarn.

Ear Flaps: Reattach yarn and work first group of 31 stitches on needle as follows: Knit 1, knit 2 together, work in eyelet rib pattern as established to last 3 stitches, knit 2 together, knit 1—*29 stitches*. Repeat this row 13 times—*3 stitches*. Bind off. Then work second ear flap in same manner on remaining group of 31 stitches on needle.

FINISHING: Weave all remaining yarn ends into back of work. Sew center back seam, working from wrong side of piece.

EDGING: Working from right side of cap, with size B crochet hook, work crab stitch edging as follows:
Round 1: Starting at center back seam, pick up and work single crochet stitches evenly around entire edge of cap, slip stitch into first stitch of round; chain 1. (*NOTE: Do not turn work.*)
Round 2: Working from left to right instead of from right to left, work 1 single crochet stitch in each stitch of previous round, slip stitch into first stitch of round; end off.
   Make ties for the cap by crocheting two 15-inch chains, using doubled strands of yarn. Sew a tie to the end of each ear flap.

BOOTEES

Beginning at upper edge of cuff, with No. 1 needles, loosely cast on 41 (41, 45) stitches. Work in garter stitch (*knit each row*) for 7 rows. Change to No. 2 needles and work in eyelet rib pattern until piece measures 2 (2, 2¼) inches, working last row on wrong side. Cut yarn.
Divide for Foot: Next Row (right side): Slip first 12 (12, 14) stitches onto a stitch holder for one side of foot; reattach yarn and work next 17 stitches in eyelet rib pattern as established; slip remaining 12 (12, 14) stitches onto a stitch holder for other side of foot.
Shape Instep: Continuing in eyelet rib pattern, work center 17 stitches until instep flap measures 2 (2, 2¼) inches, working last row on wrong side. Cut yarn.
Shape Sides and Sole: Working from right side of piece, with No. 1 needles, reattach yarn and knit the 12 (12, 14) stitches from first stitch holder, pick up 16 (18, 20) stitches along side of instep flap, place a marker on needle, knit the 17 stitches along front edge of instep flap, place a marker on needle, pick up 16 (18, 20) stitches along other side of instep flap, knit the 12 (12, 14) stitches from second holder—*73 (77, 85) stitches*. Then work even in garter stitch for 7 (7, 9) rows. (*NOTE: Keep markers in place on needle while working these rows.*)
Next Row (right side): Knit 2 together, knit to first marker, slip marker, knit 2 together, knit to 2 stitches before second marker, knit 2 together, slip marker, knit to last 2 stitches, knit last 2 stitches together—*69 (73, 81) stitches*. Work next row even in garter stitch. Repeat these 2 rows twice—*61 (65, 73) stitches*. Then work 3 rows even in garter stitch. Bind off loosely.
   Make second bootee in same manner.

FINISHING: Weave all remaining yarn ends into back of work. Sew center back and sole seams, working from wrong side of the piece. Make drawstrings for the bootees by crocheting two 15-inch chains, using doubled strands of yarn. Lace a drawstring through a row of eyelets around ankle of each bootee.

Striped Short-Sleeved Pullover, Romper and Bootees

SIZES: Directions are for size newborn–4 months. Changes for sizes 4–8, 8–12, 12–15 and 15–18 months are given in parentheses. Pullover measures approximately 18¾ (19½, 20¼, 21, 21¾) inches around chest and 12¾ (13½, 14½, 15½, 16¾) inches from shoulder to bottom edge.

MATERIALS: Baby or fingering yarn, 6 (6, 7, 7, 9) ounces navy blue, 4 (4, 4, 4, 5) ounces light green. Knitting needles Nos. 1 and 2 (or size needed to obtain gauge). Crochet hook size B. Large-eyed tapestry needle. Seven small buttons.

GAUGE: 8 stitches = 1 inch; 11 rows = 1 inch (stockinette stitch, No. 2 needles).

PULLOVER

BACK: Beginning at lower edge, with blue and No. 1 needles, cast on 78 (80, 84, 86, 90) stitches. Work even in knit 1, purl 1 ribbing for 1 inch. Change to No. 2 needles and work in stockinette stitch (*knit 1 row, purl 1 row*) for 2¼ (3, 3½, 4, 4¼) inches, finishing with a purl row. Then cut blue and work in stockinette stitch and stripe pattern as follows: 6 rows green, 6 rows blue, 6 rows green and 6 rows blue. After completing second blue stripe, change to green and work even in stockinette stitch until piece measures 5¾ (6½, 7½, 8, 9) inches or

desired length to underarm, finishing with a purl row.
Shape Raglan Armholes: Continuing in stockinette stitch with green, bind off 3 stitches at beginning of next 2 rows—*72 (74, 78, 80, 84) stitches.* Then decrease 1 stitch at each side every other row 5 times, working the decreases on the knit rows—*62 (64, 68, 70, 74) stitches.*
Divide for Center Back Opening: Next Row (wrong side): Purl first 31 (32, 34, 35, 37) stitches; drop yarn without cutting it and attach another strand of green; with new strand, purl remaining 31 (32, 34, 35, 37) stitches. Working both sides at same time with separate strands of yarn, decrease 1 stitch at each armhole edge every other row 17 (18, 20, 21, 23) times, working the decreases on the knit rows as before—*14 stitches each side.* Bind off remaining stitches on each side.

FRONT: Work as for back to underarm.
Shape Raglan Armholes: Continuing in stockinette stitch with green, bind off 3 stitches at beginning of next 2 rows—*72 (74, 78, 80, 84) stitches.* Then decrease 1 stitch at each side every other row 12 (13, 14, 15, 17) times, working the decreases on the knit rows—*48 (48, 50, 50, 50) stitches.* Purl next row.
Shape Neck: Next Row (right side): Knit first 2 stitches together, knit next 17 (17, 18, 18, 18) stitches; drop yarn without cutting it and attach another strand of green; with new strand, bind off next 10 stitches, knit to last 2 stitches, knit last 2 stitches together—*18 (18, 19, 19, 19)*

stitches each side. Working both sides at same time with separate strands of yarn, at each neck edge bind off 3 stitches once, 2 stitches once and 1 stitch 4 times; at same time, continue to decrease 1 stitch at each armhole edge every other row as before until only 2 stitches remain on each side. Bind off remaining stitches on each side.

RIGHT SLEEVE: Beginning at lower edge, with blue and No. 1 needles, cast on 45 (47, 51, 53, 57) stitches. Work even in knit 1, purl 1 ribbing for 6 rows. Then change to No. 2 needles and work in stockinette stitch and stripe pattern as follows: 6 rows green, 6 rows blue and 6 rows green; at same time, increase 1 stitch at each side every other row 6 times, working the increases on the knit rows—*57 (59, 63, 65, 69) stitches.* After completing second green stripe, cut green and attach blue to work remainder of piece.
Shape Raglan Cap: Continuing in stockinette stitch with blue, bind off 3 stitches at beginning of next 2 rows—*51 (53, 57. 59, 63) stitches.* Then decrease 1 stitch at each side every other row 20 (21, 23, 24, 26) times, working the decreases on the knit rows—*11 stitches.*
Next Row (wrong side): Purl even across row.
Next Row (right side): Bind off first 3 stitches (*front edge*), knit 5, knit last 2 stitches together—*7 stitches.*
Next Row: Purl even across row.
Next Row: Bind off first 3 stitches (*front edge*), knit 1, knit last 2 stitches together—*3 stitches.*
Next Row: Purl even across row. Bind off.

LEFT SLEEVE: Work as for right sleeve to underarm.
Shape Raglan Cap: Continuing in stockinette stitch with blue, bind off 3 stitches at beginning of next 2 rows—*51 (53, 57, 59, 63) stitches.* Then decrease 1 stitch at each side every other row 20 (21, 23, 24, 26) times, working the decreases on the knit rows—*11 stitches.*
Next Row (wrong side): Bind off first 3 stitches (*front edge*), purl remaining 7 stitches—*8 stitches.*
Next Row (right side): Knit first 2 stitches together, knit remaining 6 stitches—*7 stitches.*
Next Row: Bind off first 3 stitches (*front edge*), purl remaining 3 stitches—*4 stitches.*
Next Row: Knit first 2 stitches together, knit 2—*3 stitches.* Bind off.

FINISHING: Weave all remaining yarn ends into back of work. Block pieces lightly if necessary. Working from wrong side, sew sleeves to front and back sections. Then sew side and sleeve underarm seams.

NECKBAND: Working from right side of garment, with blue and No. 1 needles, pick up 79 (81, 83, 87, 91) stitches around neck edge. Work even in knit 1, purl 1 ribbing for 8 rows. Bind off loosely in ribbing from wrong side of work.
 Sew three yarn loops evenly spaced along one edge of center back opening. Sew buttons in position along opposite edge of opening.

ROMPER

BACK: Beginning at lower edge of crotch, with blue and No. 2 needles, cast on 16 (18, 20, 22, 24) stitches. Work in stockinette stitch (*knit 1 row, purl 1 row*), increasing 1 stitch at each side of first 34 (34, 35, 35, 36) rows—*84 (86, 90, 92, 96) stitches.* Then decrease 1 stitch

at each side every inch 3 times—*78 (80, 84, 86, 90) stitches.* Work even until side edges measure 4¼ (4½, 5, 5½, 5¾) inches, finishing with a purl row.
Shape Back (Short Rows): Row 1: Knit first 70 (72, 76, 78, 82) stitches, turn (*do not work last 8 stitches of row*).
Row 2: Slip first stitch, purl next 61 (63, 67, 69, 73) stitches, turn (*do not work last 8 stitches of row*).
Row 3: Slip first stitch, knit next 53 (55, 59, 61, 65) stitches, turn (*do not work last 16 stitches of row*).
Row 4: Slip first stitch, purl next 45 (47, 51, 53, 57) stitches, turn (*do not work last 16 stitches of row*).
Row 5: Slip first stitch, knit next 37 (39, 43, 45, 49) stitches, turn (*do not work last 24 stitches of row*).
Row 6: Slip first stitch, purl next 29 (31, 35, 37, 41) stitches, turn (*do not work last 24 stitches of row*).
Row 7: Slip first stitch, knit next 21 (23, 27, 29, 33) stitches, turn (*do not work last 32 stitches of row*).
Row 8: Slip first stitch, purl next 13 (15, 19, 21, 25) stitches, turn (*do not work last 32 stitches of row*).
Row 9: Slip first stitch, knit across to end of row, working each slipped stitch together with stitch directly below it.
Row 10: Purl across entire row, working each remaining slipped stitch together with stitch directly below it—*78 (80, 84, 86, 90) stitches.* Then cut blue, attach green and work even in stockinette stitch and stripe pattern as follows: 6 rows green, 6 rows blue, 6 rows green and 6 rows blue. Now change to green for remainder of piece and work even in stockinette stitch until side edges measure 6½ (7, 7¾, 8½, 9¼) inches or desired length to underarm, finishing with a purl row.
Shape Armholes: Continuing in stockinette stitch, bind off 7 (8, 8, 9, 9) stitches at beginning of next 2 rows, 3 stitches at beginning of next 2 rows, 2 stitches at beginning of next 2 rows and 1 stitch at beginning of next 8 rows—*46 (46, 50, 50, 54) stitches.*
Shape Neck: Next Row (right side): Knit first 16 (16, 17, 17, 18) stitches; drop yarn without cutting it and attach another strand of green; with new strand, bind off next 14 (14, 16, 16, 18) stitches, knit to end of row—*16 (16, 17, 17, 18) stitches each side.* Working both sides at same time with separate strands of yarn, at each neck edge bind off 3 stitches once, 2 stitches once and 1 stitch 5 times— *6 (6, 7, 7, 8) stitches each side.* Then work even on both sides until armholes measure 3½, (4, 4, 4¼, 4½) inches. Bind off remaining stitches on each side.

FRONT: Beginning at lower edge of crotch, with blue and No. 2 needles, cast on 16 (18, 20, 22, 24) stitches. Work even in stockinette stitch for 24 (26, 28, 28, 30) rows. Increase 1 stitch at each side of next 6 rows—*28 (30, 32, 34, 36) stitches.* Then cast on 28 (28, 29, 29, 30) stitches at end of next 2 rows—*84 (86, 90, 92, 96) stitches.* Continue working in stockinette stitch, decreasing 1 stitch at each side every inch 3 times—*78 (80, 84, 86, 90) stitches.* Then work even in stockinette stitch until side edges of piece measure 4¼ (4½, 5, 5½, 5¾) inches, finishing with a purl row. Cut blue, attach green and work even in stockinette stitch and stripe pattern as follows: 6 rows green, 6 rows blue, 6 rows green and 6 rows blue. Now change to green for remainder of piece and work even in stockinette stitch until side edges measure same length as side edges of back to underarm, finishing with a purl row.
Shape Armholes: Continuing in stockinette stitch, bind off 7 (8, 8, 9, 9) stitches at beginning of next 2 rows, 3 stitches at beginning of next 2 rows, 2 stitches at begin-

ning of next 2 rows and 1 stitch at beginning of next 8 rows—*46 (46, 50, 50, 54) stitches.*

Shape Neck: Next Row (right side): Knit first 16 (16, 17, 17, 18) stitches; drop yarn without cutting it and attach another strand of green; with new strand, bind off next 14 (14, 16, 16, 18) stitches, knit to end of row—*16 (16, 17, 17, 18) stitches each side.* Working both sides at same time with separate strands of yarn, at each neck edge bind off 3 stitches once, 2 stitches once and 1 stitch 5 times—*6 (6, 7, 7, 8) stitches each side.* Then work even on both sides until armholes measure 3½ (4, 4, 4¼, 4½) inches. Bind off remaining stitches on each side.

FINISHING: Weave all remaining yarn ends into back of work. Block pieces lightly if necessary. Working from wrong side, seam front and back sections together at crotch.

LEG RIBBING: Working from right side of garment, with blue and No. 1 needles, pick up 73 (77, 81, 85, 89) stitches around edge of one leg. Work even in knit 1, purl 1 ribbing for 1½ inches. Bind off loosely in ribbing. Repeat around edge of other leg. Sew side seams, working from wrong side of garment. Then fold each leg ribbing in half to wrong side and loosely stitch bound-off edge in place.

ARMHOLE RIBBING: Working from right side of garment, with blue and No. 1 needles, pick up 89 (93, 97, 101, 105) stitches around edge of one armhole. Work even in knit 1, purl 1 ribbing for 6 rows. Bind off in ribbing. Repeat around edge of other armhole.

NECKLINE RIBBING: Working from right side of garment, with blue and No. 1 needles, pick up 77 (81, 85, 89, 93) stitches around front neck edge. Work even in knit 1, purl 1 ribbing for 6 rows. Bind off in ribbing. Repeat around back neck edge.

SHOULDER EDGING: With blue and size B crochet hook, work 2 rows of single crochet stitches across end of each front shoulder strap. Repeat across end of each back shoulder strap; but this time, on second row, work two evenly spaced chain-stitch buttonhole loops on each strap. Then sew two buttons in position on each front shoulder strap.

BOOTEES

Beginning at upper edge of cuff, with green and No. 1 needles, loosely cast on 38 (40, 42, 44, 46) stitches. Work even in knit 1, purl 1 ribbing for 6 rows. Change to No. 2 needles and stockinette stitch (*knit 1 row, purl 1 row*) and work in stripe pattern as follows: 6 rows blue, 6 rows green and 6 rows blue. Then cut blue, attach green and work in stockinette stitch for 2 rows, finishing with a purl row.

Divide for Foot: Next Row (right side): Continuing in stockinette stitch with green, bind off first 12 (12, 13, 13, 14) stitches for one side of foot, knit remaining stitches—*26 (28, 29, 31, 32) stitches.*

Next Row (wrong side): Bind off first 12 (12, 13, 13, 14) stitches for other side of foot, purl remaining stitches—*14 (16, 16, 18, 18) stitches.*

Shape Instep: Continuing in stockinette stitch, work the 14 (16, 16, 18, 18) stitches remaining on needle until instep flap measures 2¾ inches. Bind off.

Shape Sides and Sole: Working from right side of piece, with blue and No. 1 needles, pick up 11 (11, 12, 12, 13) stitches along bound-off edge of first side of foot, pick up 16 (17, 18, 20, 21) stitches along side of instep flap, place a marker on needle, pick up 12 (14, 14, 16, 16) stitches along front edge of instep flap, place a marker on needle, pick up 16 (17, 18, 20, 21) stitches along other side of instep flap, and then pick up 11 (11, 12, 12, 13) stitches along bound-off edge of other side of foot—*66 (70, 74, 80, 84) stitches.* Work even in garter stitch (*knit each row*) for 7 (7, 9, 9, 11) rows. (*NOTE: Keep markers in place on needle while working these rows.*)

Next Row (right side): Knit 2 together, knit to first marker, slip marker, knit 2 together, knit to 2 stitches before second marker, knit 2 together, slip marker, knit to last 2 stitches, knit last 2 stitches together—*62 (66, 70, 76, 80) stitches.* Work next row even in garter stitch. Repeat these 2 rows 3 (3, 4, 4, 4) times—*50 (54, 54, 60, 64) stitches.* Then work 2 rows even in garter stitch. Bind off loosely.

Make second bootee in same manner.

FINISHING: Weave all remaining yarn ends into back of work. Sew center back and sole seams, working from wrong side of piece. Make drawstrings for the bootees by crocheting two 15-inch chains, using doubled strands of blue yarn. Using a blunt-tipped tapestry needle, weave a drawstring in and out of each bootee around the ankle.

Striped Short-Sleeved Pullover

SIZES: Directions are for size newborn–4 months. Changes for sizes 4–8, 8–12, 12–15 and 15–18 months are given in parentheses. Pullover measures approximately 18¾ (19½, 20¼, 21, 21¾) inches around chest and 9¾ (11, 12½, 13¼, 14) inches from shoulder to bottom edge.

MATERIALS: Baby or fingering yarn, 4 (4, 4, 4, 6) ounces royal blue, 2 (2, 2, 4, 4) ounces green, 2 ounces white. Knitting needles Nos. 1 and 2 (or size needed to obtain gauge). Large-eyed tapestry needle. Three small buttons.

GAUGE: 8 stitches = 1 inch; 11 rows = 1 inch (stockinette stitch, No. 2 needles).

STRIPE PATTERN: With blue and No. 2 needles, work in stockinette stitch (*knit 1 row, purl 1 row*) for 14 rows; with green and No. 1 needles, work in garter stitch (*knit each row*) for 6 rows; with white and No. 1 needles, work in garter stitch for 6 rows. Repeat these 26 rows for stripe pattern, cutting and joining colors as needed.

BACK: Beginning at lower edge, with green and No. 1 needles, cast on 78 (80, 84, 88, 90) stitches. Work even in knit 1, purl 1 ribbing for 1 inch. Change to stripe pattern, using No. 2 needles for the blue stripes and

No. 1 needles for the green and white stripes, and work even until piece measures 5¾ (6½, 7½, 8¼, 9) inches or desired length to underarm, working last row on wrong side. Then change to blue and No. 2 needles, and work remainder of piece in stockinette stitch as follows:

Shape Raglan Armholes: With blue, bind off 3 stitches at beginning of next 2 rows—*72 (74, 78, 82, 84) stitches.* Then decrease 1 stitch at each side every 4 rows 4 (5, 6, 7, 8) times, working the decreases on the knit rows—*64, (64, 66, 68, 68) stitches.*

Divide for Center Back Opening: Next Row (wrong side): Purl first 32 (32, 33, 34, 34) stitches; drop yarn without cutting it and attach another strand of blue; with new strand, purl remaining 32 (32, 33, 34, 34) stitches. Working both sides at same time with separate strands of yarn, continue in stockinette stitch, except work the 2 stitches on each side of center back opening in garter stitch (*knit on all rows*); at same time, decrease 1 stitch at each armhole edge every other row 16 times, working the decreases on the knit rows—*16 (16, 17, 18, 18) stitches each side.* Bind off remaining stitches on each side.

FRONT: Work as for back to underarm.
Shape Raglan Armholes: Working in stockinette stitch with blue and No. 2 needles, bind off 3 stitches at

48

beginning of next 2 rows—*72 (74, 78, 82, 84) stitches.* Now decrease 1 stitch at each side every 4 rows 4 (5, 6, 7, 8) times, working the decreases on the knit rows—*64 (64, 66, 68, 68) stitches.* Then decrease 1 stitch at each side every other row 7 times, working the decreases on the knit rows—*50 (50, 52, 54, 54) stitches.* Purl next row.

Shape Neck: Next Row (right side): Knit first 2 stitches together, knit next 15 stitches; drop yarn without cutting it and attach another strand of orange; with new strand, bind off next 16 (16, 18, 20, 20) stitches, knit to last 2 stitches, knit last 2 stitches together—*16 stitches each side.* Working both sides at same time with separate strands of yarn, at each neck edge bind off 3 stitches once, 2 stitches once and 1 stitch 3 times; at same time, continue to decrease 1 stitch at each armhole edge every other row as before until only 2 stitches remain on each side. Bind off remaining stitches on each side.

RIGHT SLEEVE: Beginning at lower edge, with green and No. 1 needles, cast on 44 (44, 48, 50, 52) stitches. Work even in knit 1, purl 1 ribbing for 6 rows. Change to stripe pattern, using No. 2 needles for the blue stripes and No. 1 needles for the green and white stripes; and at same time increase 1 stitch at each side every 3 rows 6 times—*56 (56, 60, 62, 64) stitches.* Then work even in stripe pattern until piece measures 2 (2, 2¼, 2½, 2½) inches, working last row on wrong side.

Shape Raglan Cap: Continuing in stripe pattern as established, bind off 3 stitches at beginning of next 2 rows—*50 (50, 54, 56, 58) stitches.* Now decrease 1 stitch at each side every 4 rows 8 (8, 10, 11, 12) times, working the decreases on the right side of the piece—*34 stitches.* Then decrease 1 stitch at each side every other row 10 times, working the decreases on the right side of the piece—*14 stitches.*

Next Row (wrong side): Work even in stripe pattern across row.

Next Row (right side): Bind off first 4 stitches (*front edge*), work in stripe pattern to last 2 stitches, work last 2 stitches together—*9 stitches.*

Next Row: Work even in stripe pattern across row.

Next Row: Bind off first 4 stitches (*front edge*), work in stripe pattern to last 2 stitches, work last 2 stitches together—*4 stitches.*

Next Row: Work even in stripe pattern across row. Bind off.

LEFT SLEEVE: Work as for right sleeve to underarm.

Shape Raglan Cap: Continuing in stripe pattern as established, bind off 3 stitches at beginning of next 2 rows—*50 (50, 54, 56, 58) stitches.* Now decrease 1 stitch at each side every 4 rows 8 (8, 10, 11, 12) times, working the decreases on the right side of the piece—*34 stitches.* Then decrease 1 stitch at each side every other row 10 times, working the decreases on the right side of the piece—*14 stitches.*

Next Row (wrong side): Bind off first 4 stitches (*front edge*), work remaining 9 stitches in stripe pattern—*10 stitches.*

Next Row (right side): Work first 2 stitches together, work remaining 8 stitches in stripe pattern—*9 stitches.*

Next Row: Bind off first 4 stitches (*front edge*), work remaining 4 stitches in stripe pattern—*5 stitches.*

Next Row: Work first 2 stitches together, work remaining 3 stitches in stripe pattern—*4 stitches.* Bind off.

FINISHING: Weave all remaining yarn ends into back of work. Block pieces lightly if necessary. Working from wrong side, sew sleeves to front and back sections. Then sew side and sleeve underarm seams.

NECKBAND: Working from right side of garment, with blue and No. 1 needles, pick up 79 (81, 83, 85, 87) stitches around neck edge. Work even in knit 1, purl 1 ribbing for ½ inch. Bind off in ribbing from wrong side of work.

Sew three yarn loops evenly spaced along one edge of center back opening. Sew buttons in position along opposite edge of opening.

Striped Long-Sleeved Pullover

SIZES: Directions are for size newborn-4 months. Changes for sizes 4–8, 8–12, 12–15 and 15–18 months are given in parentheses. Pullover measures approximately 18¾ (19½, 20¼, 21, 21¾) inches around chest and 9¾ (11, 12½, 13¼, 14) inches from shoulder to bottom edge.

MATERIALS: Baby or fingering yarn, 6 (6, 6, 7, 7) ounces orange, 2 ounces white, 2 ounces yellow. Knitting needles Nos. 1 and 2 (or size needed to obtain gauge). Large-eyed tapestry needle. Three small buttons.

GAUGE: 8 stitches = 1 inch; 11 rows = 1 inch (stockinette stitch, No. 2 needles).

STRIPE PATTERN: With orange and No. 2 needles, work in stockinette stitch (*knit 1 row, purl 1 row*) for 14 rows; with white and No. 1 needles, work in garter stitch (*knit each row*) for 6 rows; with yellow and No. 1 needles, work in garter stitch for 6 rows. Repeat these 26 rows for stripe pattern, cutting and joining colors as needed.

BACK: Beginning at lower edge, with orange and No. 1 needles, cast on 78 (80, 84, 88, 90) stitches. Work even in knit 1, purl 1 ribbing for 1 inch. Change to stripe pattern, using No. 2 needles for the orange stripes and No. 1 needles for the white and yellow stripes, and work even until piece measures 5¾ (6½, 7½, 8¼, 9) inches

or desired length to underarm, working last row on wrong side. Then change to orange and No. 2 needles, and work remainder of piece in stockinette stitch as follows:

Shape Raglan Armholes: With orange, bind off 3 stitches at beginning of next 2 rows—*72 (74, 78, 82, 84) stitches.* Then decrease 1 stitch at each side every 4 rows 4 (5, 6, 7, 8) times, working the decreases on the knit rows—*64 (64, 66, 68, 68) stitches.*

Divide for Center Back Opening: Next Row (wrong side): Purl first 32 (32, 33, 34, 34) stitches; drop yarn without cutting it and attach another strand of orange; with new strand, purl remaining 32 (32, 33, 34, 34) stitches. Working both sides at same time with separate strands of yarn, continue in stockinette stitch, except work the 2 stitches on each side of center back opening in garter stitch (*knit on all rows*); at same time, decrease 1 stitch at each armhole edge every other row 16 times, working the decreases on the knit rows—*16 (16, 17, 18, 18) stitches each side.* Bind off remaining stitches on each side.

FRONT: Work as for back to underarm.
Shape Raglan Armholes: Working in stockinette stitch with orange and No. 2 needles, bind off 3 stitches at beginning of next 2 rows—*72 (74, 78, 82, 84) stitches.* Now decrease 1 stitch at each side every 4 rows 4 (5, 6,

50

7, 8) times, working the decreases on the knit rows—*64 (64, 66, 68, 68) stitches*. Then decrease 1 stitch at each side every other row 7 times, working the decreases on the knit rows—*50 (50, 52, 54, 54) stitches*. Purl next row.

Shape Neck: Next Row (right side): Knit first 2 stitches together, knit next 15 stitches; drop yarn without cutting it and attach another strand of orange; with new strand, bind off next 16 (16, 18, 20, 20) stitches, knit to last 2 stitches, knit last 2 stitches together—*16 stitches each side*. Working both sides at same time with separate strands of yarn, at each neck edge bind off 3 stitches once, 2 stitches once and 1 stitch 3 times; at same time, continue to decrease 1 stitch at each armhole edge every other row as before until only 2 stitches remain on each side. Bind off remaining stitches on each side.

RIGHT SLEEVE: Beginning at lower edge, with orange and No. 1 needles, cast on 43 (43, 45, 45, 45) stitches. Work even in knit 1, purl 1 ribbing for 2¼ inches. Then change to No. 2 needles and work in stockinette stitch, increasing 1 stitch at each side every 6 rows 9 (9, 10, 11, 12) times—*61 (61, 65, 67, 69) stitches*. Work even until piece measures 7 (7½, 8¼, 9, 9¾) inches or desired length to underarm, finishing with a purl row.

Shape Raglan Cap: Continuing in stockinette stitch, bind off 4 stitches at beginning of next 2 rows—*53 (53, 57, 59, 61) stitches*. Now change to stripe pattern, using No. 2 needles for the orange stripes and No. 1 needles for the white and yellow stripes; and at same time decrease 1 stitch at each side every 4 rows 8 (8, 10, 11, 12) times, working the decreases on the right side of the piece—*37 stitches*. Then continue in stripe pattern and at same time decrease 1 stitch at each side every other row 10 times, working the decreases on the right side of the piece—*17 stitches*.

Next Row (wrong side): Work even in stripe pattern across row.

Next Row (right side): Bind off first 5 stitches (*front edge*), work in stripe pattern to last 2 stitches, work last 2 stitches together—*11 stitches*.

Next Row: Work even in stripe pattern across row.

Next Row: Bind off first 5 stitches (*front edge*), work in stripe pattern to last 2 stitches, work last 2 stitches together—*5 stitches*.

Next Row: Work even in stripe pattern across row. Bind off.

LEFT SLEEVE: Work as for right sleeve to underarm.

Shape Raglan Cap: Continuing in stockinette stitch, bind off 4 stitches at beginning of next 2 rows—*53 (53, 57, 59, 61) stitches*. Now change to stripe pattern and at same time decrease 1 stitch at each side every 4 rows 8 (8, 10, 11, 12) times, working the decreases on the right side of the piece—*37 stitches*. Then continue in stripe pattern and at same time decrease 1 stitch at each side every other row 10 times, working the decreases on the right side of the piece—*17 stitches*.

Next Row (wrong side): Bind off first 5 stitches (*front edge*), work remaining 11 stitches in stripe pattern—*12 stitches*.

Next Row (right side): Work first 2 stitches together, work remaining 10 stitches in stripe pattern—*11 stitches*.

Next Row: Bind off first 5 stitches (*front edge*), work remaining 5 stitches in stripe pattern—*6 stitches*.

Next Row: Work first 2 stitches together, work remaining 4 stitches in stripe pattern—*5 stitches*. Bind off.

FINISHING: Weave all remaining yarn ends into back of work. Block pieces lightly if necessary. Working from wrong side, sew sleeves to front and back sections. Then sew side and sleeve underarm seams.

NECKBAND: Working from right side of garment, with orange and No. 1 needles, pick up 79 (81, 83, 85, 87) stitches around neck edge. Work even in knit 1, purl 1 ribbing for ½ inch. Bind off in ribbing from wrong side of work.

Sew three yarn loops evenly spaced along one edge of center back opening. Sew buttons in position along opposite edge of opening.

Striped Football-Style Pullover with Long or Short Sleeves

SIZES: Directions are for size 3 months. Changes for sizes 6, 9, 12, 15 and 18 months are given in parentheses. Pullover measures approximately 18 (18¾, 19½, 20¼, 21, 21¾) inches around chest and 10¼ (10¾, 11¾, 12½, 13¼, 14) inches from shoulder to bottom edge.

MATERIALS: Baby or fingering yarn: for long-sleeved pullover, 4 (4, 4, 6, 6, 6) ounces orange, 2 (2, 2, 4, 4, 4) ounces light green, 2 (2, 2, 2, 2, 4) ounces yellow; for short-sleeved pullover, 4 (4, 4, 6, 6, 6) ounces orange, 2 (2, 2, 2, 4, 4) ounces light green, 2 ounces yellow. Knitting needles No. 3 (or size needed to obtain gauge). Sixteen-inch circular knitting needle No. 2. Large-eyed tapestry needle.

GAUGE: 15 stitches = 2 inches (garter stitch, No. 3 needles).

NOTE: Pullover is worked entirely in garter stitch (*knit each row*), the rows running horizontally on lower front and back sections and vertically on the top and sleeves. Directions for working the lower front and back sections are the same for both the long- and the short-sleeved versions of the pullover. The top and sleeve portion is worked in one piece from lower edge of right sleeve to

lower edge of left sleeve, and separate directions are given for the long- and the short-sleeved versions.

LOWER BACK: Beginning at lower edge, with orange and No. 3 needles, cast on 68 (72, 76, 78, 82, 84) stitches. Work even in garter stitch for 4 (4¼, 5, 5½, 6¼, 6½) inches and then cut orange. Now work even in garter stitch and stripe pattern as follows, cutting and joining colors as needed: ¾ inch yellow, ¾ inch green and ¾ inch orange. Bind off all stitches.

LOWER FRONT: Work same as for lower back.

LONG-SLEEVED TOP: Beginning at lower edge of right sleeve, with orange and No. 3 needles, cast on 60 (62, 66, 72, 74, 78) stitches. Work even in garter stitch and stripe pattern as follows, cutting and joining colors as needed: ¾ inch orange, ¾ inch green, ¾ inch yellow, 3½ (4, 4¼, 4½, 5, 5½) inches green, ¾ inch yellow, ¾ inch green and ¾ inch orange. Then cut orange, attach yellow and work even in garter stitch for ¼ (⅜, ½, ¾, 1, 1¼) inches, working last row on wrong side (*finish at lower front edge*).

Shape Neck: Next Row (right side): Continuing in garter stitch with yellow, knit first 24 (25, 27, 30, 31, 33) stitches (*front section*); drop yarn without cutting it and attach another strand of yellow; with new strand, bind off next 12 stitches, knit to end of row (*back section*)—*24 (25, 27, 30, 21, 33) stitches each section.* Working both front and back sections at same time with separate strands of yarn, decrease 1 stitch at each neck edge every other row 3 times, working the decreases on the right side of the piece—*21 (22, 24, 27, 28, 30) stitches each section.* Then work even on both sections at same time for 4¼ (4½, 5, 5½, 5¾, 6¼) inches, working last row on wrong side (*finish at lower front edge*). Now increase 1 stitch at each neck edge every other row 3 times, working the increases on the right side of the piece—*24 (25, 27, 30, 31, 33) stitches each section.*

Next Row (wrong side): Knit even across back section, cut yarn; knit even across front section, finishing at lower front edge.

Join for Left Shoulder and Sleeve: Next Row (right side): With remaining strand of yellow, knit even across front section, cast on 12 stitches, knit even across back section—*60 (62, 66, 72, 74, 78) stitches.* Work even in garter stitch for ¼ (⅜, ½, ¾, 1, 1¼) inches and then cut yellow. Now work even in garter stitch and stripe pattern as follows, cutting and joining colors as needed: ¾ inch orange, ¾ inch green, ¾ inch yellow, 3½ (4, 4¼, 4½, 5, 5½) inches green, ¾ inch yellow, ¾ inch green and ¾ inch orange. Bind off.

SHORT-SLEEVED TOP: Beginning at lower edge of right sleeve, with green and No. 3 needles, cast on 60 (62, 66, 72, 74, 78) stitches. Work even in garter stitch for 2¼ (2¼, 2¾, 2¾, 3, 3) inches and then cut green. Now work even in garter stitch and stripe pattern as follows, cutting and joining colors as needed: ¾ inch yellow, ¾ inch green and ¾ inch orange. Then cut orange, attach yellow and work even in garter stitch for ¼ (⅜, ½, ¾, 1, 1¼) inches, working last row on wrong side (*finish at lower front edge*).

Shape Neck: Next Row (right side): Continuing in garter stitch with yellow, knit first 24 (25, 27, 30, 31, 33)

stitches (*front section*); drop yarn without cutting it and attach another strand of yellow; with new strand, bind off next 12 stitches, knit to end of row (*back section*)—*24 (25, 27, 30, 31, 33) stitches each section.* Working both front and back sections at same time with separate strands of yarn, decrease 1 stitch at each neck edge every other row 3 times, working the decreases on the right side of the piece—*21 (22, 24, 27, 28, 30) stitches each section.* Then work even on both sections at same time for 4¼ (4½, 5, 5½, 5¾, 6¼) inches, working last row on wrong side (*finish at lower front edge*). Now increase 1 stitch at each neck edge every other row 3 times, working the increases on the right side of the piece—*24 (25, 27, 30, 31, 33) stitches each section.*

Next Row (wrong side): Knit even across back section, cut yarn; knit even across front section, finishing at lower front edge.

Join for Left Shoulder and Sleeve: Next Row (right side): With remaining strand of yellow, knit even across front section, cast on 12 stitches, knit even across back section—*60 (62, 66, 72, 74, 78)* stitches. Work even in garter stitch for ¼ (⅜, ½, ¾, 1, 1¼) inches and then cut yellow. Now work even in garter stitch and stripe pattern as follows, cutting and joining colors as needed: ¾ inch orange, ¾ inch green, ¾ inch yellow and 2¼ (2¼, 2¾, 2¾, 3, 3) inches green. Bind off.

FINISHING: Weave all remaining yarn ends into back of work. Block pieces lightly if necessary. Working from wrong side, sew lower front and back sections to top section of pullover as shown in the photograph. Then stitch side and sleeve underarm seams.

NECKBAND: Working from right side of garment, with orange and No. 2 circular needle, pick up approximately 130 stitches evenly spaced around neck edge, starting and ending at center back. Place a marker on needle after picking up last stitch of round. Work even in knit 1, purl 1 ribbing for 6 rounds, slipping marker at end of each round. Bind off in ribbing.

DOVER BOOKS ON QUILTING, CROCHET, KNITTING AND OTHER AREAS

THE UNITED STATES PATCHWORK PATTERN BOOK, Barbara Bannister and Edna P. Ford. (23243-3) $2.75

STATE CAPITALS QUILT BLOCKS, Barbara Bannister and Edna Paris Ford (eds.). (23557-2) $2.50

SMALL PATCHWORK PROJECTS, Barbara Brondolo. (24030-4) $3.50

KNITTED TOYS AND DOLLS, Nellie Burnham. (24148-3) $1.95

EASY-TO-MAKE APPLIQUÉ QUILTS FOR CHILREN, Judith Corwin. (24293-5) $3.50

DESIGN AND MAKE YOUR OWN FLORAL APPLIQUÉ, Eva Costabel-Deutsch. (23427-4) $2.50

KNIT YOUR OWN NORWEGIAN SWEATERS, Dale Yarn Company. (23031-7) $3.50

EASY-TO-MAKE FELT ORNAMENTS, Betty Deems. (23389-8) $3.00

SMOCKING, Dianne Durand. (23788-5) $2.00

EASY AND ATTRACTIVE GIFTS YOU CAN SEW, Jane Ethe and Josephine Kirshon. (23638-2) $3.50

EARLY AMERICAN PATCHWORK PATTERNS, Carol Belanger Grafton. (23882-2) $3.00

GEOMETRIC PATCHWORK PATTERNS, Carol Belanger Grafton. (23183-6) $3.25

TRADITIONAL PATCHWORK PATTERNS, Carol Belanger Grafton. (23015-5) $3.00

QUILTING MANUAL, Dolores A. Hinson. (23924-1) $3.25

NOVA SCOTIA PATCHWORK PATTERNS, Carter Houck. (24145-9) $3.50

BIG BOOK OF STUFFED TOY AND DOLL MAKING, Margaret Hutchings, (24266-8) $6.95

PATCHWORK PLAYTHINGS WITH FULL-SIZE TEMPLATES, Margaret Hutchings. (23247-6) $2.50

TEDDY BEARS AND HOW TO MAKE THEM, Margaret Hutchings. (23487-8) $6.95

THE STANDARD BOOK OF QUILT MAKING AND COLLECTING, Marguerite Ickis. (20582-7) $4.95

EASY-TO-MAKE DOLLS WITH NINETEENTH-CENTURY COSTUMES, G.P. Jones. (23426-6) $2.95

FILET CROCHET, Mrs. F. W. Kettelle. (23745-1) $1.95

FIRST BOOK OF MODERN LACE KNITTING, Marianne Kinzel. (22904-1) $3.75

SECOND BOOK OF MODERN LACE KNITTING, Marianne Kinzel. (22905-X)

Paperbound unless otherwise indicated. Prices subject to change without notice. Available at your book dealer or write for free catalogues to Dept. Needlework, Dover Publications, Inc., 180 Varick Street, New York, N.Y. 10014. Please indicate field of interest. Each year Dover publishes over 200 books on fine art, music, crafts and needlework, antiques, languages, literature, children's books, chess, cookery, nature, anthropology, science, mathematics, and other areas.

Manufactured in the U.S.A.